D1196082

MODERN WORLD NATIONS

972.93
P

C.1

The Dominican Republic

DISCARD

Douglas A. Phillips

STAUNTON PUBLIC LIBRARY

Series Editor
Charles F. Gritzner
South Dakota State University

CHELSEA HOUSE
P U B L I S H E R S
An imprint of Infobase Publishing

Frontispiece: Flag of the Dominican Republic

Cover: Guards in front of the National Palace, Santo Domingo, Domican Republic

The Dominican Republic

Copyright © 2010 by Infobase Publishing

All rights reserved. No part of this book may be reproduced or utilized in any form or by any means, electronic or mechanical, including photocopying, recording, or by any information storage or retrieval systems, without permission in writing from the publisher. For information, contact:

Chelsea House
An imprint of Infobase Publishing
132 West 31st Street
New York NY 10001

Library of Congress Cataloging-in-Publication Data
Phillips, Douglas A.
  The Dominican Republic / Douglas A. Phillips and Charles F. Gritzner.
    p. cm. — (Modern world nations)
  Includes bibliographical references and index.
  ISBN 978-1-60413-618-0 (hardcover : alk. paper) 1. Dominican Republic—Juvenile literature. I. Gritzner, Charles F. II. Title. III. Series.

  F1934.2.P47 2010
  972.93—dc22
                              2009046536

Chelsea House books are available at special discounts when purchased in bulk quantities for businesses, associations, institutions, or sales promotions. Please call our Special Sales Department in New York at (212) 967-8800 or (800) 322-8755.

You can find Chelsea House on the World Wide Web at
http://www.chelseahouse.com

Text design by Takeshi Takahashi
Cover design by Alicia Post
Composition by EJB Publishing Services
Cover printed by Bang Printing, Brainerd MN
Book printed and bound by Bang Printing, Brainerd MN
Date printed: April 2010
Printed in the United States of America

10 9 8 7 6 5 4 3 2 1

This book is printed on acid-free paper.

All links and Web addresses were checked and verified to be correct at the time of publication. Because of the dynamic nature of the Web, some addresses and links may have changed since publication and may no longer be valid.

Table of Contents

The Dominican Republic

1

Introduction to the Dominican Republic

For many readers, the Dominican Republic means but one thing—baseball players! It is true that on a per capita basis, no place in the world produces more highly skilled professional baseball players than does this small Caribbean country. But the Dominican Republic offers so much more. In this book, you will learn why the "D.R." is a hotbed of baseball. But you will also learn many other things that make the island nation such a fascinating and unique land.

LOCATION

The Dominican Republic, located on the island of Hispaniola, is one of nearly 20 countries within the Caribbean Basin. The island and country are bordered by the Atlantic Ocean to the north and Caribbean Sea to the south. Relative to the United States, the Dominican Republic is located about 750 miles (1,200 kilometers) southeast

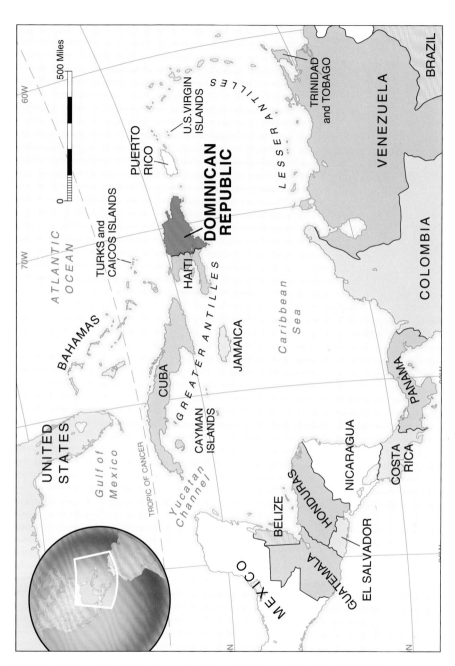

The Dominican Republic shares the island of Hispaniola with Haiti. It is the second-largest Caribbean nation, with an area of 30,242 square miles (48,670 square kilometers), which is slightly more than twice the size of New Hampshire.

of Miami, Florida. Collectively, the huge archipelago (island chain) of which it is a part is called the West Indies. It is one of the large islands that make up the Greater Antilles. Cuba and Jamaica lie a short distance to the west, separated by the Windward Passage (strait). (A chain of much smaller islands extends from off the Venezuelan coast northward as an arc to the islands lying to the east of Puerto Rico. Collectively, this group is called the Lesser Antilles.) Hispaniola is the second largest island within the Caribbean. Only Cuba is larger. It is one of only two Caribbean islands that is shared by two countries (the other being Saint Martin). Densely populated and impoverished Haiti occupies the western one-third of Hispaniola. The Dominican Republic occupies the eastern two-thirds of the island.

A COUNTRY OF EXTREMES

Among Caribbean island countries, the Dominican Republic stands out in many ways. Its area of about 18,800 square miles (48,700 square km) is second only to that of Cuba. With nearly 10 million people, its population also is exceeded only by that of its larger neighbor across the Windward Passage. Economically, its gross domestic product (GDP) also trails only that of Cuba among Caribbean nations. And its capital and largest city, Santo Domingo, is the second largest urban center in the region—behind Havana, Cuba. As a growing Caribbean tourist destination, the Dominican Republic also ranks second, in this category, behind leading Puerto Rico.

There are several categories in which the Dominican Republic ranks number one among its Caribbean neighbors. As mentioned, on a per capita basis it is far and away the world's leading producer of professional baseball players. It also has the highest mountain, the lowest spot of dry land, and the largest lake in the Caribbean. Pico ("Peak") Duarte rises to an elevation of 10,417 feet (3,175 meters), a giant among Caribbean mountains. About 80 miles (128 km) to the southwest, the Enriquillo

Basin plunges to an elevation of 151 feet (46 m) below sea level, the lowest point of dry land in the Caribbean Basin. Much of the basin floor is occupied by Lago ("Lake") Enriquillo, which covers an area of more than 100 square miles (260 square km), making it the largest lake in the Caribbean region. Because it occupies a basin of interior drainage (all water flows in and none flows out), its water is saline (salty).

It is in terms of history that the Dominican Republic really stands out among countries within the New World. (The "New World" is composed of the Americas, Australia, and Oceania. These are the places that were "discovered" during the fifteenth and sixteenth century European Voyages of Discovery.) In late 1492, Christopher Columbus landed on the island of Hispaniola, which he called La Española. His first settlement, located on the north coast of present-day Haiti, ended in tragic failure. The following year, in 1493, the Spaniards founded a settlement on the south side of the island, and they have been there since. This makes the Dominican Republic the oldest permanently settled European land in the Americas. The Dominican Republic's capital, Santo Domingo, which was founded in 1496, holds the distinction of being the oldest permanently settled European community in the Americas. The country also is home to the oldest university in the Americas and, by far, the largest college in the West Indies.

DIVERSE LANDS AND PEOPLE

Geographically, the Dominican Republic is a land of diverse natural environments and people. Land features of the island offer a variety of terrain. In fact, roughly half of the country is marked by rugged uplands and high mountains, with the other half being relatively flat low-lying valleys or coastal plains.

Hispaniola, as is true of all Caribbean islands, lies within the tropics. Some would say the balmy climate creates a tropical paradise. Temperatures are warm throughout the year and lack extremes. In the Dominican Republic and, in fact, throughout the Caribbean region, sharp climate changes occur during the rainy season. The high sun (summer) period is the wet season; during the low sun (winter) time of year, conditions are quite dry. (Because seasonal temperature changes are insignificant, within the tropics summer and winter really do not exist as we know them in the middle latitudes—the areas between the tropics and the Arctic and Antarctic.) Plant life responds to seasonal availability of moisture, with much of it becoming dried or dormant during the dry season.

Throughout much of the year, and particularly the wet season, humidity is high, which makes the weather feel muggy. This condition is somewhat countered, however, by the steadily blowing northeast trade winds. The constant breeze tends to keep temperatures in the pleasant range in terms of how people actually feel. If one wants to escape the heat, it is always possible to drive into the mountains, where temperatures are much cooler and more pleasant. Surprisingly, during the summer months, conditions are much more pleasant in the Dominican Republic than they are throughout much of the United States. In fact, tourism, which once was almost exclusively a winter event, has become a year-round activity. The warm sun, beautiful sandy beaches, off-shore coral reefs, and pounding surf lure tens of thousands of tourists to the island each year.

Besides the varied landscape, the island has a mosaic of features and cultural backgrounds that contribute to the Dominican Republic's richly diverse population. When the Spaniards arrived in the Caribbean, they "discovered" a region that had been settled by Native peoples, the Taino, for thousands of years. As was true throughout the Caribbean, Spaniards sought riches from the earth. Much of the early Spanish attention turned toward the region's mineral wealth: gold, silver, and other metals. But the Spanish and other Europeans, particularly the British and French, also established a plantation-based agricultural economy. Sugar cane, in particular, brought tremendous wealth to plantation owners. Still, the Europeans had no taste for hard labor under—to them, at least—humid, tropical conditions.

The Dominican Republic has the second-largest economy in the Caribbean. Earnings from tourism fueled this economic growth, overtaking agriculture as the leading employer of Dominicans. Ecotourism, sports and recreation, arts and culture, and the country's fascinating history have helped make the country the Caribbean's largest tourist destination.

Furthermore, besides bringing colonization to the island, the arriving Europeans brought diseases, which took a terrible toll on the Taino. Left with a shortage of labor to work the fields, Europeans imported slaves from Africa. Today, most Dominicans are of mixed ancestry, representing the biological and cultural blending that is so typical of the Caribbean region.

INSTITUTIONAL INSTABILITY

The success or failure of any country is based upon how well its institutions function. If people work together as a common society with unified goals, a firm foundation exists upon which other institutions can build. (This is the idea of nationality; one's nationality is how he or she identifies himself or herself.

In the United States, for example, regardless of biological, ethnic, or former country of origin, most people identify themselves as American.) A stable government that is responsive to the people and their needs is a second essential ingredient to the success of a country. People must be equally protected by laws. And they must be free to pursue their own goals and develop their individual potentials (within the limits of the law, of course). Finally, if people can work together within the framework of a protective government responsive to their needs, the economy will thrive.

Unfortunately, these three essential elements of success have failed to evolve in the Dominican Republic. From the very outset of European settlement, society was sharply divided between rich and poor, powerful and powerless. More often than not, one's position was determined by a caste system (organization of classes within a society). Spaniards were at the top of the socioeconomic ladder and those of African ancestry languished at the bottom.

Throughout its five centuries of European history, the Dominican Republic rarely has enjoyed political stability. Only during recent decades has some form of political stability begun to take root. As this has occurred, the economy has begun to develop accordingly. For perhaps the first time in its long history, the Dominican Republic has established a foundation upon which the country and its people can begin to realize their full potential.

CHAPTER 2

Physical Landscapes

T he natural environment forms the foundation upon which all human societies depend for their survival. This is not to say that nature determines the way people live within a particular natural setting. To the contrary, a people's culture, or their way of life, is determined by human ingenuity—what they have learned and are able to do. Much of human progress, in fact, has been marked by people learning to do things in environments that would suggest such activities were not possible.

What nature does is present an array of options to which a people must culturally adapt if they are to survive. The environment also presents options in terms of natural resources—things that people can use to their advantage. Finally, humans modify the environments in which they live in numerous ways, some good and others bad. Think for a moment about the area in which you live. How have humans culturally adapted to the environment? For example, is there artificial heating or cooling, farming or grazing of livestock, or the mining of resources? In what way are the natural elements—water, soil, vegetation, animal life, minerals, and so forth—used to human advantage? Finally, how has the natural environment in your area been changed by human activity?

Hispaniola, of which the Dominican Republic occupies the eastern two-thirds, is a tropical island. (*Tropical* is defined solely on the basis of temperature. A tropical location is one in which the average temperature of the coolest month is above 64.4°F [18°C].) Here, temperatures change very little from season to season, and frost is unknown other than at the highest mountain elevations. Under natural conditions, vegetation consists of dense tropical rain forest or, in areas of seasonal precipitation, savanna grasslands with interspersed stands of palms and other drought-resistant trees. Because of large amounts of precipitation, surface water is plentiful and tropical soils are heavily leached (emptied) of nutrients by heavy rains and are generally poor. The exception is in those locations where soils are alluvial in origin; that is, the soil and its materials have been picked up and deposited over time by flowing water, as in a valley or on a coastal plain.

The environment of the Dominican Republic offers few serious challenges to human habitation. Weather is warm and moist; valley and coastal plain soils are adequate; woodlands abound in upland areas; there are some useful mineral resources; fresh water is abundant; and the island is surrounded by the sea and its bounty. These same conditions are what attracted the first settlers. On Hispaniola, man-made changes to the various natural elements have been damaging in many ways. In the Dominican Republic, however, the natural environment has not been devastated to the degree it has in Haiti. Still, its landscape shows the negative results of human activity, particularly in terms of deforestation, the widespread extinction of native fauna, and soil erosion.

LAND FEATURES

Land features of the Dominican Republic can be described in three words: mountains, valleys, and plains. Approximately one-half of the country is upland terrain that supports little economic activity, few communities, and a low rural population density. Access is limited by few and poor transportation linkages. The great majority of human settlement, transportation networks, agriculture, manufacturing, and other economic activities are located in lowland valleys and plains. In mountainous areas, temperatures are cooler at high elevations, and in a tropical environment, uplands afford a healthier and more pleasant environment. In a poor country such as the Dominican Republic, however, little money is available to build costly roads to provide access to rugged mountainous areas. Therefore, only recently has the country been able to begin developing the tourist potential of its highlands.

Highlands

The Dominican Republic has five major mountain ranges and several smaller upland areas that run in a general northwest to southeast direction. In the northwest, the Cordillera Septentrional (Northern Mountain Range) hugs the coast. It extends from near the Haitian border to the Samaná Peninsula. To the east, the Cordillera Oriental (Eastern Mountain Range) also parallels the country's northeastern coast. Together, these mountains form a barrier to the prevailing northeast trade winds. As the winds blow upslope, they release much of their moisture on the windward side of the uplands. This condition contributes to lush tropical landscapes in many locations along the northern coast.

Inland, occupying the west central portion of the country, is the towering Cordillera Central (Central Mountain Range). These mountains form the backbone of Haiti and extend eastward into the Dominican Republic. Not only is the Cordillera Central the highest range in the Dominican Republic, but it is

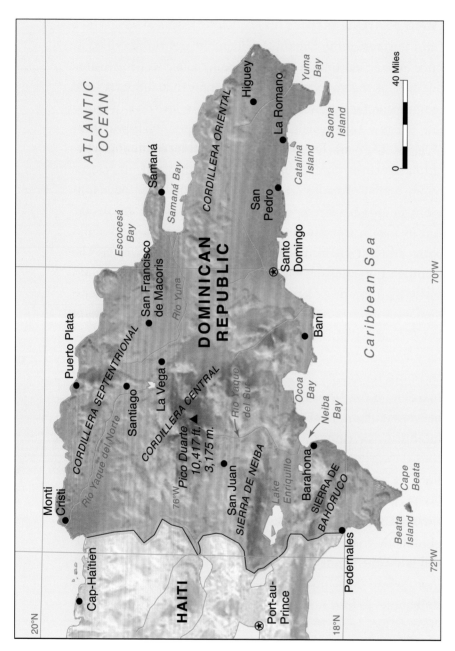

The Dominican Republic is home to sugar plantations, four major rivers, many lakes and lagoons, and five important mountain ranges. Although the climate year-round is tropical—earning it the nickname "the endless summer"—temperatures as low as 32°F (0°C) are possible in the mountains.

the highest in all the West Indies. Pico Duarte, at 10,417 feet (3,175 m), lies in the Cordillera Central range and is the highest island summit in the entire Caribbean region. Three other peaks in the range also reach a higher elevation than do any other mountains in the Caribbean. They are La Pelona (10,150 ft/3,094 m), La Rucilla (10,000 ft/3,049 m), and Pico Yaque (9,100 ft/2,760 m). The range is a major center of mining activity that includes nickel, iron, and gold production.

Two other mountain ranges are tucked away in the southwestern corner of the Dominican Republic, south of the Cordillera Central and San Juan Valley. The Sierra de Neiba is the northernmost of the two ranges. To the south, across the Enriquillo Basin, is the Sierra de Bahoruco, which also extends eastward from Haiti. The Sierra de Bahoruco is largely uninhabited because of its inaccessibility. Roads skirt the mountains but do not cross the range. Because of their remoteness, the mountains have played an interesting historical role. After the arrival of Spaniards, *alzados* (rebellious Amerindians) sought refuge in their rugged terrain. Later, escaped slaves (*maroons* in English; *cimarrones* in Spanish) also found refuge in the mountainous region.

Valleys and Plains

Narrow valleys occupy the area lying between the various mountain ranges. The most important is the Cibao Valley, or "El Cibao," which stretches between the northern and central mountain ranges. Here are the country's richest soils, most-productive agriculture, and second-largest city, Santiago. Between the Cordillera Central and Sierra de Neiba is the semi-arid and less fertile San Juan Valley. Still farther south, between the Sierra de Neiba and Sierra de Bahoruco, is the Enriquillo Basin. This valley is unusual in several ways. First, much of it is below sea level. With an elevation of –151 feet (–46 m), it is the lowest spot in the entire Caribbean Basin. Second, it is one of the hottest, most arid, and most desertlike environments in the entire Caribbean region. Finally, Lake Enriquillo, which occupies the bottom of the depression, is the largest lake within the West Indies.

The largest plains area of the Dominican Republic, the Llano Costero del Caribe (Caribbean Coastal Plain) stretches along much of the south coast. Rural settlement is rather dense, and much of the region supports sugar plantations and savanna grasslands used for the grazing of cattle.

Other Land Features

Several islands lie off the Dominican coast. Saono Island faces Mona Passage off the southeastern tip of the country and is a national park. Smaller Beata Island lies off the southernmost tip of southwestern Dominican Republic. The country also has many splendid beaches, including pure white sands that are a tourist favorite.

WEATHER AND CLIMATE

First-time travelers to the Dominican Republic who expect to find the entire island a tropical paradise will be in for a surprise. Although the country is located in the tropical latitudes, roughly between 17 and 20 degrees north latitude its climate is surprisingly varied. The climate is tropical and sunny most of the time, but portions of the south coast are almost desertlike, making the air hot and sticky. In the mountains, temperatures are quite cool and pleasant—certainly colder than one would expect for a tropical isle.

Patterns and Conditions

Overall, the country experiences a seasonally wet-and-dry tropical climate. Temperatures change very little from month to month, but rainfall is sharply divided between rainy and dry seasons. Much of the time it is very muggy because of the high humidity, which makes the air feel warmer than it really is.

Several factors account for weather patterns in the Dominican Republic and elsewhere in the Caribbean basin. Although the Dominican Republic is your typical tropical paradise, with lots of sun and very few clouds, the weather can be complicated at times based on location. Also, in the Caribbean, the seasons are marked by differences in rainfall rather than temperature. As is true throughout the Caribbean region, precipitation is seasonal. The wet season occurs during the high sun season. During the low sun period, conditions are quite dry. May through October is the rainy season, with November through April being the driest period. On average, the country receives about 50 to 60 inches (127 to 152 centimeters) of rainfall annually. But in a mountainous land such as the Dominican Republic, "average" conditions mean little. On the windward (wind-facing) northeastern mountain slopes, more than 100 inches (2,500 mm) of rain fall annually in some locations. The moisture contributes to lush tropical vegetation and a tropical landscape that has not been disturbed by human settlement. On the rain-shadow (drier, downwind) side of the various mountain ranges, conditions are quite dry. Some locations, particularly along the country's southwestern border with Haiti, receive a scant 25 to 30 inches (63.5 to 76.2 cm) of rainfall each year.

Because of its insular (island) condition, extremely hot or cold temperatures do not occur in the Dominican Republic. The Caribbean is a region bathed by the almost constantly blowing northeast trade winds, which have a cooling effect identical to what happens when one is in front of a fan on a hot day. In terms of wind and precipitation, the Dominican Republic lies squarely in the path of tropical storms. Hurricanes are rather frequent and often violent as they sweep across the island.

Weather Conditions

Weather is the day-to-day condition of the atmosphere; it is what is happening in terms of temperature, humidity, precipitation, and wind. For the country as a whole, the temperature averages around 77°F (25°C). In the lowland areas where nearly all Dominicans live, temperatures seldom rise above 90°F (32°C) or fall below 60°F (16°C). Only in the mountain towns does the temperature occasionally drop below freezing.

Conditions in the capital, Santo Domingo, are rather typical of the island's lowland seasonal temperature patterns. In July and August, the warmest months of the year, daytime highs average 88°F (31°C) and lows 73°F (23°C). During January, the coolest month, high and low temperatures average a still-balmy 84°F (29°C) and pleasant 66°F (19°C). It is often said that "nighttime is the winter of the tropics." This is because, in the tropics, day-to-night changes in temperature are much greater than those from season to season. Surprisingly, although tropical, the Dominican Republic and much of the rest of the Caribbean is cooler and more pleasant during the summer months than roughly one-half of the United States's lower 48 states. What once was a winter vacation season is now virtually a year-round event.

PLANT AND ANIMAL LIFE

Human activity has drastically changed the flora and fauna of Hispaniola. In fact, today it is difficult to know what prehuman conditions were like on the island. Certainly much of the natural vegetation is long gone, as is most native wildlife. And domestic animals far outnumber native wildlife both in variety and numbers.

An estimated one-third of the country is covered by forests, mostly in the mountainous areas. High mountain slopes support a dense forest composed primarily of pine trees. In the northeast, rainy windward slopes and lowlands support a dense growth of tropical rain forests with 27 different climate zones, resulting in an incredible variety of vegetation. There are several species of trees, such as mahogany, logwood, and lignum vitae (also called guayacan). In the interior, under natural conditions, tall savanna grasses and scattered clusters of palm trees thrive. Drier areas of the country, in the south and southwest, support semiarid savanna and dryland scrub.

Along the coast, tidal mudflats support dense stands of mangrove with its maze of stiltlike roots. Mangrove forms a distinctive and valuable coastal ecosystem. Because of its elevated and tightly enmeshed root system, mangrove protects the coastal zone from erosion. This is particularly important in a place like the Dominican Republic, which is prone to tropical storms and their resultant raging surf. The roots also provide a protective environment for many marine organisms. They include oysters, shrimp, and lobsters, fingerlings (young fish), and a host of other life forms such as algae, sponges, and barnacles. Many of the organisms that thrive within the mangrove roots form an important link in the coastal food chain.

Before humans arrived on Hispaniola, the island was home to abundant and rather varied wildlife. More than two dozen land mammals were native to the island, including monkeys, sloths, hutia (a large rodent), and the very strange Hispaniolan solenodon (a very large shrew). Few places in the world, however, have experienced a higher rate of land species extinction during the historic period. When people and wildlife are in conflict, it seems that humans always win. Of the original species, only the hutia and solenodon remain. There are, of course, many birds, insects, and both fresh- and saltwater species. The island also is home to several nonvenomous snakes and alligators that are found in some rivers. Most animals, however, were introduced by Europeans. They include domesticated dogs, cats, and pigs, as well as rats and mongooses, the latter having been brought from India.

There is one wild animal that deserves special mention. The weird Hispaniolan solenodon is one of the world's rarest and strangest living creatures. In appearance, the solenodon is quite small, about the size of a large rat. It has a stocky body, tapered claws, and a long snout somewhat resembling that of an anteater. But what makes it unusual is that although the solenodon is an insectivore, it is one of a very small number of venomous mammals. Venom is injected snakelike through grooved teeth. The shrewlike creature has endured for more than 75 million years, but scientists fear that it is now on the verge of extinction. The strange creature has all but disappeared from neighboring Haiti, but a small population continues to exist in the Dominican Republic. Efforts are now being made to ensure its survival.

WATER FEATURES

Several dozen rivers drain the various Dominican uplands. The largest is the Yaque del Norte, which flows from east to west down the Cibao Valley and into Monte Cristi Bay in the country's northwest corner. Other important streams include the Yuna, Ozana, and Artibonito. Several dams provide hydroelectric power.

The country's largest inland water feature is Lake Enriquillo, a saltwater body that occupies the lowest part of the below-sea-level Enriquillo Basin. With dimensions of 9 to 12 miles (15 to 20 km) and covering an area of 102 square miles (265 sq km), Enriquillo is the largest lake in the West Indies. Other sizeable lakes include Laguna de Rincón (also called Cabral), the country's largest freshwater lagoon, and Laguna de Oviedo, a brackish lagoon. Both lagoons are located in national parks and both feature a variety of birds, including herons and flamingos, native turtles, and other wildlife.

NATURAL HAZARDS

Because the Dominican Republic lies in the middle of the Atlantic hurricane belt, June through November is a dangerous time for the citizens of the country. This is called hurricane season, and September is usually the most active month for hurricanes in the Caribbean. A hurricane is a tropical storm with winds in excess of 74 miles per hour (119 km per hour). In addition to damaging winds, such storms often are accompanied by torrential rains. Along coasts, storm surges—wind-pushed walls

Hurricane season in the North Atlantic runs from June 1 to November 30, with September statistically being the peak month. Although the Dominican Republic sits in an area that is prone to hurricanes, historically, hurricanes have been widely spaced out in years. When they do occur, the major storms have caused catastrophic damage and millions of deaths. This photo shows the aftermath of a hurricane in Boca de Yuma.

of water—can cause severe flooding and extensive damage to coastal structures and fields.

Due to these severe storms, the Dominican Republic experiences periodic flooding but also—at the opposite extreme—occasional droughts. These treacherous storms, which move in a generally east-to-west direction across the Atlantic, have struck the country on numerous occasions, often with devastating results. In May 2004, more than 20 inches (50.8 cm) of rain fell over a period of several days. Particularly heavy rainfall occurred in the southwestern mountainous region of the country. Several hundred people lost their lives as a result of flash flooding and mudslides. Crops and transportation infrastructure, such as bridges and roadways, were washed away.

Along with death and destruction, hurricanes can bring economic ruin. In the Dominican Republic, much of the housing, particularly in rural areas, is quite flimsy. Structures are not able to withstand hurricane-force winds. Sugarcane and palm trees are extremely vulnerable to high winds and are easily destroyed. Storm-related flooding causes extensive damage, as do mudslides that can destroy buildings, roadways, and fields. Several storms in particular have devastated the Dominican Republic.

In 1930, the island of Hispaniola was struck by one of the most deadly hurricanes on record. Hurricane San Zenon hit the Dominican Republic with winds of up to 150 miles per hour (240 km per hr). More than 8,000 people lost their lives, including some 2,000 fatalities in Santo Domingo alone. About half of the capital city was destroyed. Many decades later, this violent storm still ranks as the fifth deadliest ever to strike the Caribbean.

Hurricane David struck the country with incredible force in 1979. Winds were clocked at 175 mph (280 km per hr), which made David a rare Category 5 hurricane. Nearly 1,000 lives were lost in the Dominican Republic and 70 percent of the country's crops were wiped out by the storm's fury.

In 1998, Hurricane Georges raked the Caribbean and made a direct hit on the Dominican Republic. The storm's toll was extraordinary. Winds exceeded 120 miles per hour (195 km per hr) at times, and up to 40 inches (101.6 cm) of rain fell on portions of the country. Rivers overflowed their banks, flooding many cities, rural homes, and fields. When the storm passed, 438 people were confirmed dead or missing; 500,000 Dominicans were injured; and more than 155,000 people were left homeless, including 10 percent of the population of Santo Domingo. Trees were snapped or uprooted, and power lines were down, resulting in a complete power blackout throughout the country. Mudslides covered miles of roadway, and 70 percent of the country's bridges were destroyed, resulting in a massive loss of the country's transportation infrastructure. Some mountain communities were cut off from the outside world for weeks. Ninety percent of all plantations were destroyed, and the crop loss ran well over 50 percent. Some estimates placed the direct economic loss to the island at more than $6 billion. The long-term losses, such as those from a huge drop in tourist revenue, were much greater.

A TROPICAL PARADISE

Generally speaking, the natural environment poses few obstacles and offers numerous opportunities to the people of the Dominican Republic. The terrain offers many developmental options, ranging from good farmland to cool, mountainous landscapes. The coastal zone, with sun, sand, and surf, is appealing. Because the country is on the margin of the tropics, neither temperatures nor precipitation are extreme. The developmental problems that the Dominicans have faced are more the result of human failure than of environmental challenges or limitations.

CHAPTER

3

The Dominican Republic Through Time

S tudying the history of a place is an important process. It helps to examine the various pieces and elements that have come together to form the country and culture being examined—in this case the Dominican Republic. What are these pieces? They range from the first peoples who inhabited the island to the outside influences that swept in and changed the indigenous culture in new and different ways—some good and some not so good. The land is a part of the story, too. It sets the stage on which the stories of the Dominican people have been played out through time.

LOOKING BACK

A walk through the streets of Santo Domingo provides a quick and informative introduction to the Dominican Republic's past. The sights, sounds, smells, and tastes all provide insights into the rich past of the country and its culture. Passing the El Faro a Colon monument, where many say the bones of Christopher Columbus are buried, one cannot help but be gripped by a deep sense of history. Another street shows an impressive structure called the Alcazar de Colon, which was built for Diego, the son of Columbus, who was appointed the colony's governor in 1509. In this building, Diego greeted history-making explorers like Vasco Núñez de Balboa, Hernán Cortés, and Ponce de Leon. Each building seems to tell a story, with some buildings dating back nearly 500 years.

The sounds also yield insight into the Dominican Republic's past. Spanish is heard almost everywhere, but it is spoken differently than in Spain. Local inflections and dialects are evident and provide evidence of Taino (the native Amerindian tongue) and African influences, along with a tinge of Haitian Creole. English is also commonly heard, perhaps from tourists or local vendors, which shows the connections that have developed with the United States and Canada.

The smells of the nearby sea and local foods tantalize visitors and Dominicans. Foods on the streets of Santo Domingo include American influences such as McDonald's, KFC, Burger King, Domino's, and Pizza Hut. More revealing of the country's past, however, are the numerous local vendors and restaurants whose foods reflect the deeper Spanish, Taino, and African cultural elements. Some of the foods are as simple as fresh fruit sold by a street vendor or a coconut with a hole punched in it and a straw inserted from which one drinks the juice inside. This walk has provided only a few of the puzzle pieces that can be found in the capital city. This chapter will further investigate the history of the country and its people.

THE FIRST DOMINICANS

Pre-Columbian Dominicans are believed to have emigrated from the Amazon region of South America more than 5,000 years ago. These people were ancestors of the Arawak Indian

The Taino migrated to the Caribbean from the Orinoco River Valley in South America 1500 years before Spanish explorers arrived. Although European colonization devastated the Taino communities in the Dominican Republic, Taino heritage can still be found in the country's language, food, festivals, family traditions, agriculture, and spiritual beliefs. Above is a Taino petroglyph site in a shallow cave beside Lake Enriquillo.

people who settled on Hispaniola, bringing their language, also known as Arawak. The name these people called themselves was Taino, which meant "good" or "noble."

In addition to Hispaniola, the Taino also had settled in Jamaica, Cuba, and Puerto Rico. The Taino lived in villages with a chief as the head of the tribe. People in the tribe paid tribute to the chief, who was called a *cacique*. Chiefs inherited their position. Five major tribes existed and lived harmoniously with one another. Most men practiced polygamy, or had two or three wives. The cacique, however, often had as many as 30 wives. The wives of the cacique were held in high prestige in the patriarchal Taino society. The cacique and his family usually had a large home, whereas common people might have nearly 100 people living together in a round house called a *bohio*. These buildings were constructed with wooden poles, straw, and palm fronds (leaves). As many as 15 families would live in a single bohio.

Agriculture was very important. Most Taino lived by farming but also were involved in fishing and hunting small mammals, ducks, and turtles. Cassava (manioc) was an important crop and was baked into flat bread. Other agricultural products included corn, hot peppers, beans, squash, and sweet potatoes. According to some historians, the Taino population on the island had reached 1.5 million to 3 million by the time the Spanish arrived. This number would change dramatically after the Europeans settled on Hispaniola.

The Taino religion was polytheistic, meaning that they believed in many gods. Their gods were called *zemi* and were often depicted in stone-carved idols. These gods were believed to control different parts of the universe, much like the Greeks once believed with their gods. One important zemi was called Yucahu. This god was the spirit of the cassava plant, which was very important and served as a mainstay in the Taino diet. The cacique and priests would use the zemi idols to contact the gods for advice and assistance. People would use body piercings and tattoos as expressions of their faith. Festivals with dancing, worship, and healing practices were often held to celebrate Taino religious beliefs. Some of these festival practices have had a lasting impact upon Dominican festivals today.

Isolated for centuries and protected by the seas, the Taino had enjoyed a very good life, and the population had increased to its highest levels. All of this was destined to change radically right before the dawn of the sixteenth century.

ARRIVAL OF THE EUROPEANS

As is commonly known, Christopher Columbus "discovered" America on October 12, 1492. His landfall is believed by most geographers and historians to have been on one of the outer Bahamas, perhaps San Salvador (Watling Island). Columbus and his crew were greeted by Native peoples who had found and settled the Americas thousands of years earlier. Poor Columbus, in fact, was quite lost. The Native American population bears evidence of the explorer's gigantic geographical mistake. Even today, they are known as "Indians." Why? Because Columbus believed that he had reached the East Indies (today's Indonesia and its neighboring islands)—a location half the world away.

After exploring the Bahamas and Cuba, on December 5, 1492, Columbus reached the north shore of a large island that he named La Isla Española (Hispaniola). There, along the northern coast of present-day Haiti, he decided to build a small fort from which he and his men could lay claim to the island for the Spanish crown. Because these events occurred around Christmas Day, Columbus named the fort La Navidad. Once the fort was built, Columbus left about 40 men at the garrison and sailed back to Spain. Upon his return to the Caribbean in November 1493—with 17 ships and about 1,200 men—he found La Navidad in ruins and no sign of survivors. It is assumed that the settlers were killed by Taino warriors, but their actual fate remains a mystery.

Columbus decided to rebuild nearby and named the town Isabella in honor of the Spanish queen. It became the first

Spanish colony in the Americas. Yet the site proved to be unsatisfactory. After three years along the north coast, Columbus decided to move his settlement to the drier leeward (downwind, or south) side of the island.

In 1496, Columbus, his brother Bartholomew, and his men founded yet another town, Nueva (New) Isabella. But it, too, was short-lived. The settlement was destroyed by a hurricane, so its inhabitants rebuilt it at a new site across the Ozama River. This town was named Santo Domingo de Guzmán and today is known as Santo Domingo. The new settlement would serve the Spaniards well. It became the capital and center of their colonial operations in the New World, a position that it held for nearly a century. In fact, Santo Domingo holds the distinction of being the oldest continuously settled European community in the New World. (It should be noted that there are many Native American communities that have been continuously settled for a much longer time.)

According to geographer Carl O. Sauer, the Santo Domingo-based colony established the pattern for all subsequent Spanish colonization of the New World. In Sauer's words:

> It began with trade, including ornaments of gold. The quest for gold brought forced labor and the dying-off of the natives, and this, in turn, slave-hunting and the importation of black slaves. Decline of natives brought food shortages and wide abandonment of conucos [small native farm plots]. Cattle and hogs were pastured on the lately tilled surfaces; and Spaniards, lacking labor to do gold-placering, became stock ranchers.... One hope of fortune failing, another was tried; the stumbling into Empire was under way by men who had scarcely any vision of founding a new homeland.

Vast differences exist between the social, economic, and political stability of North America and Latin America. Sauer's concluding comment helps us to better understand why this condition exists. Most early settlers in North America came to settle the land permanently and begin a new—and hopefully better—life. Most Spaniards, on the other hand, were soldiers of fortune. Their goal was to get rich and get back to their homeland. They paid little attention to developing those institutions and other foundations of a stable New Spain here in the New World.

According to a 1496 census taken by Bartholomew Columbus, it is estimated that the island had a population of about 1.1 million Taino Indians. The Spaniards soon enslaved them to work in the island's gold mines. It was not long before a variety of factors combined to take a dreadful toll on the Taino population. Forced labor, hunger, and the outright killing of Taino by the Spaniards resulted in the deaths of thousands. The greatest killers, however, were the various European-introduced diseases against which the Taino had no natural immunity. Within a decade of the arrival of the Spaniards, the Taino numbers had plunged to around 50,000, or between 10 and 15 percent of its former total. By 1516, the numbers were reduced to 12,000 and by 1542, there were fewer than 200 Taino. This tragic loss was repeated throughout much, if not most, of the New World.

French Interests on Hispaniola

By the dawn of the seventeenth century, Spain's interests had shifted from the Caribbean region to possessions on the mainland of the Americas. Much of the island of Hispaniola had been abandoned by Spanish settlers, who had flocked to Santo Domingo (the city and its surrounding territory). This allowed French and other European pirates to establish footholds on the island, particularly in the western portion of the island. Over the years, French influence grew to the point that, by 1665, France had gained control of a large colony named Saint-Domingue (present-day Haiti). In 1697, Spain formally ceded Saint-Domingue to France. It was not long

In 1503, the Spanish colonizers instituted the encomienda system. The conquistadors were to take responsibility in instructing the Taino in the Spanish language and in the Catholic faith, receiving in return labor, gold, or other products. The colonizers also took possession of land belonging to the Taino and abused them.

before the Spanish-held territory on Hispaniola dwindled into a social, economic, and political backwater. Meanwhile, Saint-Domingue, on the island's west end, had become the wealthiest colony in the New World.

By the late 1700s, Saint-Domingue was involved in a bloody revolution. Spain decided to take advantage of the conflict and attempted to gain control of the western portion of the island. The decision proved to be ill-advised and costly. A native-born black general, François-Dominique Toussaint L'Ouverture soundly defeated the Spanish forces. By 1795, France controlled the entire island. Thus began a half-century of animosity and political ping-pong between eastern and western powers on Hispaniola.

DOMINICAN REPUBLIC DECLARES ITS INDEPENDENCE

Saint-Domingue had fought for and won its independence in 1804 and renamed the country Haiti after one of the Taino names for the island. Now free, Haitian forces invaded the east end of the island four times in efforts to retake the whole island. Fortunately for the Dominican Republic, none of these Haitian efforts succeeded. After many unsuccessful attempts at gaining its independence, the Dominican Republic finally won its freedom on February 27, 1844. A secret Dominican society called La Trinitaria had been working toward independence since 1836. Led by Juan Pablo Duarte, a founder of La Trinitaria, the Dominicans revolted against Haitian rule.

The Dominican Republic adopted its first constitution on November 6, 1844. This document was based on the U.S. Constitution. Pedro Santana was elected as the first president of the country and served three terms. His presidency was marked by internal divisions. Some people wanted the country to return to Spanish rule, which it did briefly during the early 1860s. Others wanted the United States to take over the country. The United States did intervene during a brief period in the 1860s when Spain had once again annexed the Dominican Republic. In 1865, the second Dominican Republic was declared, and the United States forced the Spanish to withdraw. The next 14 years were marked by turmoil and instability. Between 1865 and 1869—a turbulent period of only four years—the country had no fewer than 20 presidents!

THE DOMINICAN REPUBLIC NEARLY BECOMES A U.S. TERRITORY

In 1869, the Dominican president, Buenaventura Baez, negotiated a treaty with the United States that would have had the

Dominican Republic annexed by, or become a territory of, the United States. In return, the United States would assume all of the debt of the Dominican Republic. The idea was supported by American president Ulysses S. Grant, but the treaty was not ratified (approved) by the U.S. Senate. Grant believed that annexing the Dominican Republic would give newly freed American slaves a new home in an all-black country where they would be protected. He also believed that the Dominican Republic would provide important natural resources for the U.S. economy. The opposition was led by Massachusetts Republican Senator Charles Sumner. He believed that southern blacks should be protected by the U.S. government rather than be shipped off to a new country, as many advocated. In the end, Sumner's view prevailed and the treaty failed by a single vote in the U.S. Senate.

THE END OF THE NINETEENTH CENTURY

After the treaty failed to pass, President Baez was ousted in a coup in 1878 and sent into exile to Puerto Rico. Ulises Heureaux, the son of a Haitian father and a mother from the island of St. Thomas, was handed the reins of government in 1882 for a two-year term. His term was not particularly noteworthy, because the previous administrations had achieved stability throughout the country. General Francisco Billini won the 1884 presidential election, but Heureaux spread dangerous rumors against Billini that caused him to resign. Heureaux continued to have a dominant role in government and was reelected to the presidency in 1886. He then forced Congress to change the constitution to abolish the two-year presidential term and eliminate popular elections. Although Heureaux faced no serious challenges, the Dominican Republic became a military state and the number of political prisoners expanded. He sought the protection of a foreign power, principally the United States, offering his northern neighbor the lease to the Samaná Peninsula. Although this deal failed due to opposition from European powers, in 1891, Washington and Santo Domingo concluded a treaty that allowed 26 U.S. products free entry into the Dominican market in exchange for similar duty-free access for Dominican goods. The governments of Germany, Great Britain, and France filed official protests over the treaty, stating that it harmed their most-favored-nation trading status. When awarded this status by another country, the receiving nation is granted trade advantages, such as low tariffs, that would not be awarded to any other nation. The Dominican-U.S. treaty would give both countries unfair advantages.

Heureaux's presidency was marked by economic corruption and the abuse of the presidential office to enrich Heureaux, the army, and others loyal to Heureaux. At the same time, Heureaux was pushing the country into bankruptcy as the nation's foreign debt was ballooning out of control. Many in the country viewed him as a despicable dictator, and a revolutionary organization formed to lay the groundwork for a rebellion. While the dictator passed through the town of Moca on July 26, 1899, Heureaux was fatally shot by Ramón Caceres Vasquez, a young revolutionary. Heureaux's marble tomb is located today in the cathedral at Santiago.

THE TWENTIETH CENTURY

The Dominican Republic entered the new century with overwhelming foreign debts. The late President Heureaux had left the country broke and deeply in debt to France and other foreign creditors. The French and other European nations began to pressure the Dominicans to repay their loans. The United States also had long-term interests in the country. In 1906, under President Theodore Roosevelt, the United States signed a 50-year financial agreement with the Dominican Republic. This agreement had the United States managing the Dominican Republic's customs—the country's main source of income. The U.S. administration would then use the fees to pay off the debt of the Dominican Republic. This agreement had the Americans assuming management and responsibility for much of the country's debt.

AMERICAN MILITARY RULE

Unrest continued in the decades after Heureaux's death. This resulted in the United States establishing a firm military government under the U.S. Marines from 1916 until 1924. Before this time, Dominican financial problems still existed and political instability plagued the country. The era of U.S. military rule was resented by most Dominicans, but it also had positive effects. First, the Marines restored order and brought peace to the country. Second, the United States built an effective Dominican National Guard. Third, the Dominican economy came back to life under U.S. rule. Fourth, the United States built a road system that connected all parts of the country. Fifth, and perhaps most importantly, the U.S. rule finally balanced the Dominican Republic's government budget and reduced the debt owed to other countries.

While there was some armed resistance to the U.S. occupation, the American governance didn't end until after World War I. The U.S. public had also grown tired of the Dominican occupation. Warren Harding campaigned for the U.S. presidency as an opponent of the U.S. occupation of the two countries on Hispaniola. After Harding was elected president, he ended U.S. rule in the Dominican Republic in 1924. The Dominican Republic election in 1924 installed Horacio Vásquez as the new president. The Dominican Republic was an independent country again.

FROM DEMOCRACY TO DICTATORSHIP

The first six years of Vásquez's presidency were very successful. Political and civil rights were reestablished and it was a time of economic prosperity. It was a golden age in Dominican history, with new public works and modernization projects in Santo Domingo. Tragically, this positive era in Dominican history came to a rapid end with political infighting that resulted in the election of General Rafael L.Trujillo in 1930. Trujillo was elected without opposition, as he had eliminated all potential

The Trujillo Era (1930–1961) is known as one of the bloodiest of the twentieth century. Rafael Trujillo (*center, saluting*) ruled over the Dominican Republic for more than 30 years, assigning positions to family members such as his wife, Dona Maria (*left*), and his brother, Hector (*right*), and brutally oppressing the country's citizens and border Haitians.

competitors. His election marked the start of nearly a third of a century of dictatorial rule that had Trujillo and his family controlling all important aspects of Dominican society with an iron fist.

Trujillo wasn't president for all of the 31 years that he ruled the Dominican Republic. At times he would install a puppet president, although Trujillo retained all real power. Feeding his ego, he even renamed Santo Domingo after himself with the name Ciudad Trujillo (Trujillo City). Even with his dictatorial rule, some good things did happen in the country. For example, the greatest strength of Trujillo's reign was the economic development that took place. Important foundations of Dominican society were strengthened, including education, health care, public works, and transportation. He also instituted important social programs that benefitted lower- and middle-class Dominicans and finally repaid all of the country's foreign debt. However, the damage that Trujillo did to political and civil rights was severe, as he used the military to impose and maintain his will.

Trujillo was ruthless. In 1937, over a six-day period, his troops killed 20,000 to 30,000 Haitians who were living on the Dominican side of the border. This slaughter is called the Parsley Massacre, an event that horrified people and countries around the world. The massacre was in response to a report that Haitians were stealing cattle and crops from borderland Dominicans who subsisted mostly on agriculture. Haitians were also taking farm land, which posed a possible threat to Trujillo's regime because of long-standing border disputes between the neighboring nations. From October 2 to 8, Haitians were killed with machetes, guns, clubs, and knives by Dominican troops, civilians, and local political authorities. This horrible event was called the Parsley Massacre because Trujillo had his soldiers hold up a sprig of parsley and ask citizens to identify it. If they could not pronounce the Spanish term for the word, *perejil* (*pesi* in Haitian Creole and *persil* in French), they then were identified as Haitian and killed. The genocide of Haitians was ironic in that Trujillo himself was one-fourth Haitian.

Trujillo also used an extensive secret police network to monitor and control Dominicans. Resistance to the rule of Trujillo expanded both within and outside the country as human rights violations increased. His 1960 attempt to assassinate Venezuela's president, for example, failed. He installed Joaquín Balaguer as his new puppet president in 1960. Balaguer tried to institute some political reforms, but the Trujillo era of ruling ended harshly with the dictator's assassination in May 1961. Having bled his country dry, Trujillo was one of the richest men in the world at the time of his death. The military then seized control and ousted Balaguer in 1962.

DEMOCRACY RISES AND FALLS—AGAIN AND AGAIN

After the military took over the government in 1962, free elections were held. Juan Bosch was elected president and inaugurated early in 1963; however, he was also overthrown by the military. The country then fell into economic, social, and political chaos until the United States intervened, sending the Marines to restore order. In 1966, elections once again were held, and Joaquín Balaguer was again elected president. Many accused the United States and Balaguer of election fraud, but the results stood and Balaguer was reelected twice and remained president until 1978. Other political parties did not participate in the 1970 and 1974 elections, as they believed the elections would be unfair.

Balaguer's presidency also was marked by the repression of individual freedoms and human rights abuses. Yet, he did continue to develop the country's infrastructure with roads, housing, water systems, and other projects. He also promoted land reform by redistributing lands to the poor. The United States backed Balaguer, as they saw him as a strong anti-communist who would work with them to fight communism. The United States also wanted to make certain that the Dominican Republic didn't become another Cuba, which had undergone a communist takeover in 1959 under Fidel Castro.

In the 1978 election, Balaguer was defeated by Antonio Guzmán. During Guzmán's presidency, corruption continued to be a problem. In 1982, facing charges that his family had embezzled from the government, Guzmán committed suicide. Salvador Jorge Blanco was elected president later that year. Guzmán and Blanco were members of the Dominican Revolutionary Party, and both worked to improve human rights and individual freedoms. However, both presided over a corrupt government and a declining economy. Blanco was found guilty of corruption and misuse of government funds and sentenced to 20 years in prison. Instead he sought political asylum (protection) in Venezuela. His sentence was overturned by the Dominican Supreme Court in 2001, and today he is practicing law in Santo Domingo.

BALAGUER RISES AGAIN

Joaquín Balaguer was again elected president in 1986. Opposing parties were disorganized, and Balaguer's victory brought a return of more dictatorial government. He was reelected again in 1990 and in 1994 at the age of 88. Most observers outside the Dominican Republic believed that these elections were rigged and stolen by Balaguer, a suspicion that increased international pressure on his leadership. He agreed to serve only a two-year term, and Leonel Fernandez was elected president in 1996. Balaguer died in 2002 at the age of 95 after being involved in the highest levels of government for 40 years.

Hipolito Mejia was elected president in 2000 but served only one term, as Fernandez won both the 2004 and 2008 elections. Fernandez has brought economic reform to the country and has modernized ports, roads, mass transit, and other parts of the infrastructure. Corruption is still a problem in the country, and Fernandez seems less concerned about social problems and remains more focused on economic problems and development. Another step toward progress has been taken in the twenty-first century with free and fair elections. This is in stark contrast to the Trujillo and Balaguer eras, when rigged elections were common.

Thus, the Dominican Republic has entered the new century with the strongest democratic government in the country's history. Economic problems remain but at a diminished scale. Still, further action against corruption and political incompetence is desperately needed. So is continuing development of the economy and a much improved quality of life for the country's citizens.

CHAPTER

4

People and Culture

Nearly 10 million people call the Dominican Republic home. Most of them are of mixed European and African ancestry. Most Dominicans live in cities, although much of the country's rural landscape is densely packed. In this chapter you will learn about the Dominican people. You will get a glimpse of their demographics (demography is the science involved in the study of population numbers) and settlement. You also will learn about who they are (ethnicity) and how they live (their culture, or way of life). Are you ready to meet the Dominican people?

POPULATION

The Dominican Republic has the second-largest population of any Caribbean country, at nearly 10 million people. In July 2009, its official estimated population stood at 9,650,054. According to some estimates,

Up to one million Haitians currently live in the Dominican Republic. They face extreme poverty in their homeland and cross the border to look for work, fuel, and arable land. Once there, many face discrimination and violence, including recent incidents like the May 2009 beheading of a Haitian migrant in the Dominican Republic. Still, Haitians wait in line to cross the border into the Dominican Republic, hoping for a better life in the neighboring country.

however, there may be as many as one million Haitians in the country, most of whom are undocumented (in the country illegally). So any population number is guesswork. Regardless, the country has about one million fewer people than Cuba, the most populated country in the Caribbean Basin. It also has about one million more people than its island neighbor, Haiti, which is the third most populated country in the West Indies.

Only four factors can determine whether a population grows or declines: births, deaths, in-migration, and out-migration. Using this information, there are a number of ways to measure population change. One is the annual rate of natural increase

(RNI). This figure is 1.5 percent for the Dominican Republic. It means that currently the population is growing by about 145,000 people each year as a result of there being more births than deaths. Worldwide, the figure stands at about 1.15 percent, so the Dominican population is increasing at a rate somewhat higher than the world average. In 2008, the country experienced about 22.4 births per 1,000 people and only 5.3 deaths, the latter figure being one of the world's lowest. This suggests that the country has a young and rather healthy population.

Another way of viewing population change is the total fertility rate (TFR)—the average number of children to which a woman will give birth during her fecund (fertile) lifetime. In the Dominican Republic, the figure is 2.8. This is well above the replacement rate of 2.1 (the .1 is because some people do not have children).

Migration is still another factor that contributes to population change. Because of its relatively poor economy and, until recently, poor government, the Dominican Republic has long experienced a relatively high rate of out-migration: Currently, it stands at about -2.2/1,000. This means that each year between 21,000 and 22,000 Dominicans leave their island home. Many of them move to the United States. This, of course, helps keep the population in check, despite the country's relatively high RNI and TFR.

Throughout history, people have moved about in search of a better life as often measured by economic gain. Dominicans have a per capita income that is nearly six times greater than that of their island neighbors, the Haitians. In addition to being the poorest people in the Western Hemisphere, the Haitians are also among the most crowded, with nearly 800 people per square mile (310 per square km). As a result, many Haitians, perhaps as many as one million, have migrated to the Dominican Republic, most of them illegally. At the same time, a substantial number of Dominicans flee eastward across the Mona Passage to Puerto Rico. There, as illegal immigrants, they seek better jobs and higher incomes.

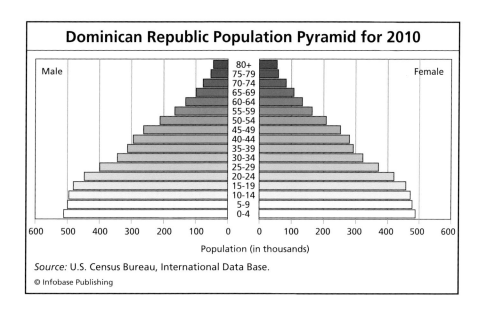

Dominican Republic Population Pyramid for 2010

Male / Female

Age groups: 80+, 75-79, 70-74, 65-69, 60-64, 55-59, 50-54, 45-49, 40-44, 35-39, 30-34, 25-29, 20-24, 15-19, 10-14, 5-9, 0-4

Population (in thousands): 600 500 400 300 200 100 0 0 100 200 300 400 500 600

Source: U.S. Census Bureau, International Data Base.

© Infobase Publishing

Yet another way of viewing a population is by its age structure. This is best done by looking at a population pyramid (see chart). As is true of most developing countries, the Dominican population is quite young. Nearly one of three residents is 14 or younger. On the other hand, only about 6 percent of the population is 65 or older. (Figures for the United States and Canada, respectively, are 20.2 and 12.8 percent that are 14 or under, and 16.1 and 15.2 percent that are 65 or older.) Overall, the Dominican population on average is just under 25 years of age (versus 37 years of age for the United States and 40 years of age for Canada).

DEMOGRAPHY AND HUMAN WELL-BEING

Various demographic data also can tell us a great deal about the well-being of a selected population. There are many different indices that experts use to determine how well off a selected population is relative to others. In Chapter 7, you will learn about the Human Development Index (HDI); it is one measure of well-being that takes into consideration a number of factors. Here, we will stick to demographic data.

Life expectancy of Dominicans—on average how long they live—is almost 74 years. This is about seven years longer than the world average. As is true nearly everywhere, women outlive men in the Dominican Republic. Life expectancy for females is nearly 76 years and for males about 72 years. Another significant indicator of a country's living standards is its infant mortality rate. This figure is a measure of deaths from birth until age one. The number is an excellent indicator of medical care, health services, sanitation, child safety, parenting, and other factors. For the Dominican Republic, the figure is 26 deaths per 1,000 live births. This places the country just about in the middle among the world's nations. But it remains quite high relative to infant mortality rates in developed lands. In the United States and Canada, for example, the figures are 6 and 5 deaths per 1,000, respectively.

SETTLEMENT

As is true throughout most of Latin America, Dominican settlement—where people live—is primarily urban. About 70 percent of the people live in cities and this figure is growing rapidly. In fact, between 2005 and 2010, it is estimated that the rate of urban population growth was about 2.6 percent. What is happening in the Dominican Republic is rather typical of trends throughout much of the developing world. Rural people—faced with poverty, inadequate or even nonexistent services, and often difficult lives—opt for better conditions in the city.

Population density is a figure that demographers, geographers, and others often use as though it has some meaning. Those of us who live in the U.S. interior know that the country's population density figure of nearly 130 people per square mile (50 per square km) is all but meaningless. Much of the Great Plains and interior West has fewer than 10 people per square mile (under 4 per square km). So, when you learn that the Dominican Republic has 509 people per square mile

According to the U.S. Agency for International Development (USAID), although the Dominican Republic has one of the fastest-growing economies, about 30 percent of its citizens live below the poverty line. Many of the rural poor move to urban areas for better opportunities, but instead face stiff competition for resources, high rates of unemployment, and increased crime.

(197 per square km) know that this does not mean that each square mile holds that many people. Some parts of the country, such as the southwestern highlands, have a very low density. Because of its isolation, very few people live there. Under existing conditions, it would be extremely difficult for them to make an adequate living in that area. On the other hand, the district surrounding Santo Domingo is home to several million people and has a very high density. For the country as a whole, however, the density is six times higher than that of the United States and a whopping 60 times higher than that of Canada.

Most Dominicans live in the large cities. The largest, by a wide margin, is Santo Domingo: Nearly three of 10 Dominicans, about 3 million people, reside within the city's urban area. Santiago de los Caballeros (usually shortened to simply Santiago), with a population of about 2 million, is the country's second-largest city. It lies in the fertile Cibao Valley in the north-central part of the Dominican Republic. Other cities with more than 100,000 people living within their urban area include La Romana, San Pedro de Macoris, San Francisco de Macoris, San Cristobal, Puerto Plata, and La Vega. Elsewhere, the rural and small-town population is scattered about, primarily in the fertile valleys and coastal plains. With few exceptions, the mountainous regions support the lowest population densities and have very few communities.

ETHNICITY

Three of every four Dominicans are of mixed ancestry, mainly black African and Spanish (Negroid and Caucasoid). The native Taino tribe was all but eliminated from Hispaniola, although some residents claim to have a small amount of Taino blood. Only about 16 percent of the population is "pure" white (if, indeed, such a concept is valid in the Dominican Republic or, for that matter, elsewhere!) and another 11 percent "pure" black. The country also has a large Haitian community with, as mentioned previously, some estimates running as high as one million people. Many, if not most, of the Haitians are illegal immigrants who came to the Dominican Republic in search of work. This is the primary source of the country's 11 percent black population. Of the 16 percent of Dominicans who claim white ancestry, most are Spanish. But there also are substantial numbers of people of German, American, Italian, Portuguese, or French heritage. Additionally, immigrants from the Middle East and elsewhere in Asia have added to the country's diversity. Thus, it is not unusual to meet Syrians, Chinese, Japanese, or Lebanese in the Dominican Republic, particularly on the streets of highly cosmopolitan Santo Domingo.

From the earliest period of settlement, the Spaniards imposed a strict social system—*la casta*—upon the island's population. Under this system, the Spanish divided society into social classes with those born in Spain being at the highest level. Following this elite class in descending order were Taino Indians, followed by *zambos* (persons of mixed Taino and African lineage), and finally black slaves who ranked at the bottom of the social structure. Many carryovers of this casta social structure are still deeply imprinted on Dominican society and culture. This has resulted in a social pattern of bias, with the elite being lighter skinned and the darker skinned being among the poor and relatively powerless. Fortunately, this pattern is beginning to change as people are becoming more tolerant of diversity.

LANGUAGE

Language and religion are other remnants of the Spanish legacy in the Dominican Republic. Spanish, also known by its local dialect, Castilian, is the country's official language. It is spoken by nearly all residents today. If you have learned textbook Spanish in school, don't assume that you could easily speak to or understand someone speaking Dominican Spanish! The language isn't necessarily the same as the Spanish spoken in Spain. Through time, the language has been "Dominicanized" through the addition of local words, meanings, and pronunciations, including many from the Arawak (Taino) language.

Other languages also can be heard in the country, including French and English. French is largely the result of the cultural spillover from neighboring French-speaking Haiti. As a result, French in the Dominican Republic is spoken with a heavy Haitian accent. English is the primary language of globalization, including tourism. Each year thousands of visitors from the United States and Canada visit the Dominican Republic.

The country wants to ensure that visitors have a pleasant travel experience, because tourism represents a significant and rapidly growing segment of the economy. Therefore, those in the tourist industry are encouraged to learn English in order to communicate with visitors. So, too, must people engaged in any type of international business, media, entertainment, communications, or sports.

RELIGION

The dominant religious affiliation of Dominicans also can be traced back to the Spanish and their Roman Catholic faith. Columbus and Spanish missionaries brought their Catholic religion with them in the fifteenth and sixteenth centuries, and the Bible was later put into the curriculum in all public schools. Even with religious freedom being practiced today in the Dominican Republic, 95 percent of the people remain Roman Catholic in their faith. There are small numbers of Protestants, animists, and those who claim no religious affiliation. Dominican animism has its roots in Africa and its practitioners believe that all living things, including plants and animals, have a spirit or soul.

DINING AND DIET

Foodways—what people eat and all of the customs associated with dining and diet—represent one of the strongest and least flexible traits of a people's culture. In the case of the Dominican Republic, the country's cuisine is like so many other aspects of its society and culture, reflecting a distinctive blend of the country's Taino, African, and Spanish heritages, with a spicy touch of other cultures thrown in. A meal may include Spanish, Taino, and African dishes at the same setting along with other foods that reflect the Dominican or regional mix of these elements.

Pork, chicken, a variety of seafoods, goat, and beef are common meat staples. Other diet staples include potatoes, sweet

Ninety percent of Dominicans continue to practice the Roman
Catholic faith, which had been introduced by Columbus and Spanish
missionaries. Nevertheless, with the influx of missionaries from foreign
countries and Haitian immigrants, the number of alternate religions
that are practiced has grown in recent years, including Afro-Caribbean
Creole religions, Judaism, Islam, Mormonism, Santeria, and voodoo.
Above is a Christian religious procession in the small town of Sosúa.

potatoes, plantains (a banana-like fruit that usually is cooked), beans, corn, and white rice. Major fruits include banana, mango, papaya, pineapple, coconut, melon, passion fruit, tomato, and a variety of citrus fruits.

As is true throughout much of the tropical realm, lunch is the most important meal of the day. The practice, although common in much cooler lands as well, is a wonderful adaptation to the intense midday tropical heat and humidity. During the heat of the day, workers take an extended break that lasts from about noon until midafternoon. (They then work well into the cooler evening.) A large and leisurely lunch is often followed by a *siesta*, or nap. This tradition comes from the Spanish, and the break is called *la bandera*. Many people believe incorrectly that the siesta is associated only with the tropics and the region's intense heat. Actually, it has little to do with weather. The practice appears to be a widespread European custom that was brought to the Caribbean during colonial days.

The Dominican national dish, relished by people at all levels of society, is *sancocho*.

Here are the ingredients (the full recipe can be found on various Internet sites; simply enter "Sancocho" for complete details):

Sancocho ingredients
Chicken
Tocino (bacon or other cured meat)
Pork chops
Goat meat
Sausage
Yucca (a root crop)
Malanga (a root crop similar to the potato)
Ears of corn
Water
Oregano
Salt
Naranja agria (bitter orange used as a marinade)

Onion
Garlic
Parsley leaves
Cilantro leaves
Chicken bouillon cube
Spanish pumpkin
Sweet potatoes
Plantain bananas
White yam or taro
White vinegar
Worcestershire sauce; optional
Green bell pepper

Like the list of ingredients, the cooking instructions for the sancocho recipe are extremely detailed and complex and go on for two pages. Just for fun, can you do some research to determine the original source of the various ingredients used in the recipe? You may be surprised to learn that few, if any, originated in the Dominican Republic. Recipes, perhaps more than any other aspect of Dominican living, illustrate the incredible richness of the country's culture.

DOMINICAN CULTURE—A UNIQUE BLEND

This chapter has explained how Dominican culture is a blend of traits contributed through time by many peoples. The original Taino people are long gone from the island of Hispaniola, but their imprint lives on in many ways. Some words we use today, such as *hammock* and *canoe*, for example, were borrowed from the Taino language. A number of crops and their use in foods also trace back to the Taino.

Spaniards contributed their language and religion, as well as certain lingering social patterns. It has been said that much of Latin America suffers from the continued influence of "sixteenth century Iberian [Spanish] cultural baggage." In many respects, this is true. The Dominican Republic is a highly polarized society, with a few very wealthy and many very poor citizens, which is a carryover from the Iberian caste system. So, too, is the kind of political stability that results from a "strong arm" head of government. Leaders of such types of governments often are far more interested in lining their pockets while in office than they are in helping their people and country prosper.

Africans, several million of whom were brought to the Caribbean as slaves to work the sugar plantations, also have made substantial contributions to the region. Their influence is evident in the physical appearance of many Dominicans. They also have contributed to the language, foodways, religions (including animism), music and other arts, and much more.

Today, Dominican culture is becoming globalized at a rapid rate. Many people, particularly in the cities, have been "Americanized." They speak English as a second language, dress in the Western style, watch and listen to American media, and are dependent upon modern technological conveniences. For example, many, if not most, Dominicans use cellphones, have television sets, and have access to the Internet.

This chapter has covered the most fundamental elements of a culture—its language, religion, and diet. Many other aspects of the Dominican way of life as they affect living today are discussed in Chapter 7.

CHAPTER

5

Government and Politics

S anto Domingo is the capital and largest city of the Dominican Republic. It has a history that stretches back more than 500 years to the time of brothers Christopher and Bartholomew Columbus. Bartholomew founded the settlement of Nueva Isabella (New Isabella) in 1496, which officially became Santo Domingo in 1498. Santo Domingo is the first city built in the New World by Europeans that has endured through time. The city served as the base for the Spanish, who used Santo Domingo as a launching pad for exploration, conquest, and settlement in lands around the Caribbean Sea. Thus, the city has served as the location for governmental leadership for more than five centuries.

With some 3 million residents in the city and its surrounding district, Santo Domingo is home to nearly a third of the country's citizens. It also is home to all three branches of the Dominican government. This includes the president's office, called the National Palace; the legislature, called the National Congress; and the highest court, which is called the Supreme Court of Justice. When looking toward the government, all eyes in the Dominican Republic turn toward Santo Domingo, the seat of the country's political power.

The government of the Dominican Republic has jurisdiction (authority) over all of the lands and people in the country. This jurisdiction includes the eastern side of Hispaniola, Saona Island, Beata Island, Alto Velo Island, and other smaller nearby islands. As the co-inhabitant of Hispaniola with the country of Haiti, that relationship is important and will be explored later in this chapter.

NEW DIRECTIONS IN GOVERNING THE DOMINICAN REPUBLIC

The government of the Dominican Republic has had some historic bumps and upheavals since its separation from Haiti and, later, Spain. These situations led the country into military rule, dictatorships, and elections tainted with unfairness and corruption—all problems that the country and its citizens have worked to correct in recent years.

The role of the military decreased in the 1960s, but political corruption and questionable elections followed until the 1990s. Finally, at the end of the twentieth century, most international observers found the country's elections to be fair and free. These new traditions are the ones that Dominicans are hoping to keep alive in the future.

THE DOMINICAN CONSTITUTION

The most fundamental law of a country is its constitution. This represents the highest law in the land and establishes the structure of government. It also provides its citizens rights and protections from the government. However, constitutions in the Dominican Republic have been fragile. In fact, there have been 32 of them, more than any other country, since it became independent in 1844. This suggests that there have been many problems and that powerful people and groups have used their influence to render past constitutions ineffective. Thus, new constitutions continued to be written in an attempt to improve the situation.

Democratic societies seek to provide and preserve the rule of law. This means that all citizens, even leaders, are expected to follow the laws of the country. This situation is not found in all societies, as many have a government in which the rule of man (a government in which rules of government and conduct are presided over by a single person or a select group of persons) prevails. This rule of man allows some powerful people to operate above the law and allows them to abuse their positions without legal consequences. This was true during the dictatorial reign of Rafael L. Trujillo, when corruption and violations of human rights were rampant. The Dominican Republic has struggled to move forward from the way things were during Trujillo's rule. The country is working to prevent the rule of man and become a modern democracy with the rule of law prevailing, but a widespread lack of respect for the rule of law is still a significant problem in the country.

The country's current constitution was adopted in 1966 and amended (changed) in 2002 to allow the president to seek a second term. This action was deemed necessary as the 1966 constitution only allowed the president to serve a single four-year term of office. The constitution establishes a legislative branch with two houses: a Senate and a Chamber of Deputies. A judicial branch also is established by the constitution. It includes the country's highest court, called the Supreme Court of Justice. Finally, the constitution creates an executive branch that is headed by the country's president.

Legislative Branch

The bicameral (two house) legislative branch has responsibility for making laws in the Dominican Republic. There are 32 members of the Senate who are elected to four-year terms of

Founded by Bartholomew Columbus in 1496, Santo Domingo is the oldest city in the Americas and the government and financial center of the country. Pictured is the National Palace, the head office of the Dominican government. Besides hosting events for dignitaries and political personalities in its impressive salons, the palace also offers guided tours to Dominican citizens as well as foreign visitors.

office by a popular vote of the citizens. The 178 members of the Chamber of Deputies also are elected to four-year terms. Elections for the two groups alternate every two years with the presidential election.

The country has a multiparty system. This means that there are many political parties that participate in the elections and in governing. It also may require different parties to work together at times to form a coalition government. The three major political parties are the conservative Dominican Liberation Party (Spanish: Partido de la Liberacion Dominicana, or PLD), the democratic socialist Dominican Revolutionary Party (Spanish: Partido Revolucionario Dominicano, or PRD), and the conservative populist Social Christian Reformist Party (Spanish: Partido Reformista Social Cristiano, or PRSC). The PLD is the party of social liberals, the PRD supports elements of both socialism and capitalism, and the PRSC is the party of business. The PLD was elected to a majority in both houses in the 2006 elections with the PRD holding the second most seats and the PRSC third. All three of these parties have held power at some time since 1966.

Judicial Branch

Courts interpret the laws and act as the final arbitrator in both criminal and civil cases. The highest court in the Dominican Republic is the Supreme Court of Justice, which has 16 justices. These justices are appointed by the National Judicial Council, which includes as members the president, the leaders of both legislative houses, the president of the Supreme Court, and others.

The Supreme Court hears cases that are appealed from lower courts, and the court also serves to manage the country's judicial system. It is the only court to have power in cases brought against the president. The court is also relatively independent, a vitally important factor that assists in rendering fair decisions.

Executive Branch

The executive branch is responsible for carrying out and enforcing the laws in the country. This branch is headed by the president, who is elected on the same ballot as the vice president for a term of four years. With the constitutional change in 2002, a president can now serve two terms in office.

During his term in office, President Fernandez has worked to update the Dominican Republic technologically. One major area of concentration is transportation. Since the beginning of 2009, a new and modern mass-transit system called "El Metro" has been operating in Santo Domingo. This subway system was the first step in implementing Fernandez's national plan for a modern transportation system. The president has also worked to expand energy sources for the country.

The cabinet assists the president in governing the country and provides leadership in many areas of government. These subdivisions are called ministries and are headed by secretaries, or ministers, who are nominated by the president. Examples of Dominican ministries include departments for the armed forces, foreign relations, finance, education, labor, public works, agriculture, and tourism.

GOVERNMENT SERVICES

Governments are responsible to their citizens and must provide a number of important services. The national government supports the armed forces and a variety of other services, including education, health care, and law enforcement. For example, in 2000, the government established universal health care insurance in an effort to improve maternal and children's health care in the country.

Many of these programs are managed by civil servants—government officials who are appointed to their position to administer the public policies of the government. Unfortunately, many of these positions, even at lower levels, are filled with political party loyalists after elections, regardless of their qualifications. This practice is called *cronyism* and it is corrupt and costly to society. Instead of carrying out their responsibilities to citizens, the appointees provide their loyalty to the person who appointed them. The social costs include reduced business opportunities for the public,

The administration of President Leonel Fernandez (*left*), pictured with Vice President Rafael Alburquerque (*right, holding flag*), has pushed for economic reform and increased participation in global forums. Under Fernandez's leadership, the Dominican Republic has seen some success, earning the trust of many citizens. Others, however, criticize his focus on technological development at the expense of education, judicial, and health reforms.

reduced competition in the marketplace, inflated prices on products, decreased economic performance, and poor workmanship in public and private projects. In contrast, lower-level civil servants in Western countries such as the United States, Canada, and the United Kingdom are not replaced after elections. This allows for effective management of government programs, increases government transparency, and decreases corruption.

LOCAL GOVERNMENTS

The Dominican Republic has local governments that have jurisdiction over and responsibility for the region they serve.

Local governments address nearby problems or services that are important to citizens such as roads, schools, and police. Until the 1960s, local governments had little power because the national government held most of the power. Local governments couldn't tax, and this factor alone limited their influence. A remedy was proposed that intended to increase the power of local governments. This gave rise to a municipal league (a union of various local reform groups) that came into existence in 1962. However, these efforts have had limited success as the old habits of national control often sabotaged efforts to move greater authority to the local levels.

Even with these limitations for local governments, the Dominican Republic now has 31 provinces and a national district, 31 municipal districts, and 95 municipalities. Each province has a governor who is appointed by the president. Santo Domingo is the national district and the capital. Each of the municipalities has a mayor and a municipal council with at least five members. The council members and mayors are elected to their positions.

THE ROLES OF THE CITIZEN

Citizens in the Dominican Republic have the responsibility to elect people to govern, along with other duties required of citizens in a civil society. Duties of the citizens identified in the country's constitution include acting in a responsible, moral, and legal manner. Citizens also are expected to protect social justice, public order, and the common good of all citizens.

The constitution provides rights and liberties to its citizens. These include equality, security, liberty, property, and other social guarantees. The constitution also provides protections for unemployment, illness, old age, and disability. Citizens have the right to vote and hold public office along with freedoms that include freedom of movement, conscience, worship, expression, association, and the freedom to work. Citizens are provided with due process, a fair way of doing things in legal processes that includes the right to defense, the presumption of innocence, and the guarantee of a hearing. Citizens have the right to an education, and a person's life is protected by law.

The Dominican Republic has also signed important international agreements designed to protect human rights in the country. These include the Universal Declaration of Human Rights, of which the Dominican Republic was one of the founding signers on December 10, 1948, and the American Convention on Human Rights, which was adopted by the nations of the Americas in 1969 and came into force on July 18, 1978. The country also ratified the International Covenant on Civil and Political Rights in 1978.

FOREIGN RELATIONS

Foreign relations focus mainly on the Caribbean region and the Americas. The close proximity of neighboring countries provides for important economic, political, and social relationships. The United States is a dominant player in the region and is a key political and economic factor in Dominican affairs. This relationship is discussed in greater depth later in this chapter.

Even with its primary relationships in the Caribbean and Americas, the Dominican Republic is active in the international community. The country belongs to many international organizations such as the United Nations, World Trade Organization, Organization of American States, World Bank, World Health Organization, International Court of Justice, and others. The country has also signed on to important international agreements including the Universal Declaration of Human Rights, Climate Change-Kyoto Protocol, Ozone Layer Protection, and the Comprehensive Nuclear Test Ban.

Many internal problems confront the country. One of these is drug smuggling, and another problem is forced labor, including sexual slavery. Many of the drugs smuggled out of the Dominican Republic end up in the United States, and people forced into prostitution or slavery end up in locations around the world, ranging from Australia to Western Europe. This is called human trafficking. Because there is a huge discrepancy among the wealthy and the poor and a high rate of unemployment, trafficking in women and children remains a serious problem. According to the U.S. State Department's 2009 Trafficking in Persons Report, a significant number of women, boys, and girls are enslaved within the country and forced into domestic servitude and prostitution, particularly in coastal resort areas. In some cases, parents push their children into this work to help support the family. Dominican officials are intensifying efforts to eliminate trafficking by educating the public about the dangers of this practice, improving government assistance to the victims, announcing a national plan to combat trafficking, and taking disciplinary action against lower-level officials suspected of participating in trafficking.

Haitian Relations

Sharing the island of Hispaniola with Haiti has proved to be difficult at times, as relations between the two countries have often been hostile. In the nineteenth century, Haiti frequently invaded the Dominican Republic and plundered the population and land during periods of occupation. Dominicans also have long held a prejudice against the darker-skinned Haitians who were viewed as African in origin and inferior. Each country has tried to influence elections and politics in the other country, and the border between the two often has been closed.

Haiti is a very poor country that lies directly to the west of the Dominican Republic. The countries share a rather porous 224 mile (360 km) border through which thousands of Haitian immigrants have crossed illegally into the Dominican Republic. Most of these Haitians are searching for work, which is hard to find in their impoverished country. The per capita income of Dominicans is nearly six times higher than that of Haitians. Not only is Haiti very poor, but the country also has nearly as many people as the Dominican Republic living in only half the amount of land. As a result, the Dominican Republic is home to an estimated one million Haitians who are not citizens; rather, they are living in the country illegally.

The Organization of American States has taken an interest in the relationship between Haiti and the Dominican Republic. In 2008, the organization urged the two countries to establish mechanisms designed to foster better relations and promote peaceful coexistence. Small actions are being taken that could lead to better and more extensive relationships. One of these efforts involves beekeepers from the two countries. In 2008, beekeepers from Haiti and the Dominican Republic got together to discuss how to reduce deforestation and pests that harm bee populations and honey production in both countries. This effort has led to agreements to cooperate on pest control of barroasis, a parasite that ravages bee populations, and to improving environmental conditions for bees.

Even with these small efforts, the relationship between Haiti and the Dominican Republic is in need of much more work. A mutual history filled with two centuries of conflicts, prejudice, and illegal immigration will not be quickly or easily resolved.

Relations with the United States and Canada

While the United States has previously interfered in Dominican political affairs, today the United States represents the most important foreign relationship with the Dominican Republic. With American tourists visiting and sometimes settling in the Dominican Republic and Dominican baseball players moving to and working in the United States, the relationships today are complex. For example, the U.S. Embassy estimates that 100,000 Americans now live in the Dominican Republic. It is estimated that more than one million Dominicans live in the United

The Dominican education system is especially lacking, with poor Dominican children having increased risk of economic and social abuse due to limited access to schooling. In April 2009, U.S. Secretary of State Hillary Clinton visited the Rosa Duarte School in Santo Domingo to announce the donation of $12.5 million from the organization USAID to allow 450 public schools to access a full range of reading, writing, and math programs and to train teachers, principals, and other staff.

States, primarily in Florida and the Northeast. The ties between these two countries come in many forms.

The two countries today have friendly relations and work together on a number of issues, including trade, drugs, and illegal immigration. Trade is extensive and U.S. investment in the Dominican Republic accounts for the largest share of outside money invested in the country. Nearly half of the country's imports come from the United States, while two-thirds of the exports are to the United States. The United States exported $6 billion to the Dominican Republic in 2007, while the Dominicans exported $4.2 billion to the United States. Much of the U.S. investment is in the apparel, footwear, and electronics industries.

In 2009, Canada and the Dominican Republic celebrated 55 years of diplomatic relations. While the relationship does not have the history and complexity of the one between the Dominican Republic and the United States, the association has been of great importance to both countries. For one, the Dominican Republic has been dependent economically on Canadian tourists, who visit the Dominican Republic to escape cold Canadian winters. In 2003, an important agreement was struck between Canada's prime minister and the Dominican president that expanded cooperation in trade, construction, power generation, and renewable energy. The Dominican Republic has been an important trading and investment partner for Canada. According to the Foreign Affairs and International Trade Canada Web site, in 2006, the Dominican Republic was Canada's fourth largest export destination for goods in the Caribbean. It was also an important destination for tourism, investment, and services. Canadian exports to the Dominican Republic totaled $163 million, and imports from the Dominican Republic to Canada totaled $114 million. Recently, the two countries initiated free-trade-agreement discussions. A successful conclusion of a two-way commercial trade agreement between them would benefit both countries, resulting in fewer barriers to trade and expanded opportunities for exporters and investors in a broad range of sectors.

A FINAL LOOK

Since Trujillo's iron-fisted dictatorship, government in the Dominican Republic has changed greatly. Today, the country has a democratic government that provides greater rights and protections for citizens than at any previous time in its history. Elections are now freer than they have ever been. Still, problems persist with the country's government. Corruption and cronyism are rampant, and the government and various public institutions lack transparency. A lack of respect for the rule of law remains an important problem that plagues the country and its citizens.

Other problems include human trafficking, illegal immigration, and drug smuggling. The tense border situation with Haiti needs serious attention; if it's resolved, both countries will greatly benefit. There is room for optimism as the government continues to work, even if slowly, toward achieving better ethics and greater transparency.

CHAPTER

6

The Dominican Republic's Economy

A country's economy is the engine that fuels its daily life and determines the well-being of its citizens. Whether it's providing transportation systems or jobs and consumer products or public services, a country's economy has a significant influence on the daily activities of citizens and is the lifeblood of a country. Thus, the health of the country's economy is vital to the Dominican Republic and its citizens.

The economy of the Dominican Republic is the second largest among Caribbean countries, trailing only Cuba. The country once was known primarily for sugar production, but today, mining, manufacturing, services, and tourism are some of the most important industries. Agriculture still makes up about 11 percent of the economy, industry another 24 percent, and services generate nearly two-thirds (65 percent) of the country's gross domestic product-purchasing

6

The Dominican Republic's Economy

A country's economy is the engine that fuels its daily life and determines the well-being of its citizens. Whether it's providing transportation systems or jobs and consumer products or public services, a country's economy has a significant influence on the daily activities of citizens and is the lifeblood of a country. Thus, the health of the country's economy is vital to the Dominican Republic and its citizens.

The economy of the Dominican Republic is the second largest among Caribbean countries, trailing only Cuba. The country once was known primarily for sugar production, but today, mining, manufacturing, services, and tourism are some of the most important industries. Agriculture still makes up about 11 percent of the economy, industry another 24 percent, and services generate nearly two-thirds (65 percent) of the country's gross domestic product-purchasing power parity (GDP-PPP). (GDP represents the total value of a country's total economic activity during a one-year period; purchasing power parity represents the amount of goods and services that a country could purchase in U.S. dollars.) In 2008, the country's GDP was estimated to have been about US$77 billion. On a per capita, or per person, basis, this works out to about $8,100 per person.

The economy has a number of challenges, including a high unemployment rate of 15.5 percent as of 2009. Inflation is another problem, as the rate grew to 12 percent per year in 2008. Hurricanes and tropical storms regularly cause severe damage to the country's economy. Other problems include a wide gap between rich and poor; a lack of energy resources such as coal, oil, and natural gas; price fluctuations for minerals and agricultural products; and illegal immigration and criminal activity, such as drug-money laundering from neighboring Haiti. In 2003, the country experienced a banking crisis when one of its largest banks collapsed, resulting in the 100 percent depreciation (loss in value) of the Dominican peso. The effects of the recent global economic recession also have severely affected the Dominican Republic.

AGRICULTURE, FISHING, AND FORESTRY

Agriculture has been an important part of the Dominican economy for centuries, because it is the part of the economy that is most consumed by the country itself. Sugar has been the traditional powerhouse in the agricultural sector, but other crops have expanded the range of farm products. These include commodities such as coffee, tobacco, cocoa, bananas, fruits, and berries. Local consumers feast on Dominican-grown plantains, potatoes, rice, beans, and cassava (a banana-like plant that serves as an important source of carbohydrates). Farm animal production includes poultry, cattle, and hogs, all of which are raised mostly for domestic use.

Despite the tremendous growth in the economy due to tourism, agriculture continues to be important to the country's development. Besides producing much of its own food, the country exports a considerable amount. Its leading cash crops are sugarcane, tobacco, and coffee, and organic bananas posted a record crop in 2009. Dominican bananas reached 23 European and Asian nations, the United States, and the Caribbean Islands.

Seawater fish caught for local consumption include tuna, mackerel, snapper, and bonito. The Atlantic blue marlin, sailfish, wahoo, and white marlin attract tourists who come for a deep-sea-fishing adventure. Still, the fishing industry has not been a leading source of revenue since deep-sea resources are too inadequate to support a highly specialized fishing industry.

The country once experienced deforestation and depletion of its forest reserves at a rapid rate. In 1990, conservation efforts were initiated. These efforts included the widespread replanting of trees and the preservation of many areas under government protection as national parks, wildlife sanctuaries, and nature reserves. Since conservation measures were introduced, the size of the country's forests has stayed about the same. Today, studies suggest that about one-third of the land is now forested with mahogany, cedar, and pine trees. Some challenges remain, however, as the earlier deforestation has caused serious soil erosion problems in portions of the country.

MINING

Since the arrival of the Spaniards five centuries ago, mining has been a traditional industry in the Dominican Republic. Gold has played a key role in the country's economy, from Spanish gold mining dating back to the 1520s to the end of the twentieth century, when the Dominican Republic possessed the Western Hemisphere's largest open-pit gold mine. Today the Dominican Republic also produces ferronickel (an alloy of iron and nickel used in the making of steel), copper, amber, gypsum, and silver.

The Western Hemisphere's largest open-pit mine, located at Pueblo Viejo and opened in 1979, was closed in 1999 due to technical, environmental, and financial difficulties. The mine, which had been operated by the government, had caused a substantial negative impact on the environment. Acid from the operations polluted streams and groundwater. Erosion problems also arose with the immense pit mine. With gold prices soaring in 2008, however, Canada's Barrick Gold Corporation announced that it would reopen the mining area in the central part of the country and agreed to assist in the cleanup of the area. Gold is expected to be mined in the fourth quarter of 2011 and is expected to result in the creation of thousands of jobs. This business effort represents the largest single foreign investment in the Dominican Republic. In addition to gold, the mine will also produce copper and silver. It is estimated that the life of the Pueblo Viejo mine will be about 25 years.

MANUFACTURING

Most of the goods manufactured in the Dominican Republic are intended for markets in North America. With the United States receiving two-thirds of the country's exports, most of the manufacturing is geared toward U.S. markets. Many of the companies making these products are owned by U.S. interests that seek to manufacture in the Dominican Republic because of cheaper labor costs and the close proximity to the United States. This second factor means that transportation costs from the Dominican Republic to the United States are less expensive than between the United States and many other cheap international producers.

Manufactured goods include clothing, footwear, electronic components, glassware, and leather goods. Much of the assembly work in these industries is done by women. Other important industries include sugar refining and the production of cement, steel, rum, and cigarettes. More than 200,000 Dominicans are employed in the country's various manufacturing industries.

TOURISM AND THE SERVICE INDUSTRY

The Dominican Republic has become the Caribbean's largest tourist destination. Visitors to the island come by air or cruise ships to visit the country's beautiful beaches and historic sites, to see winter baseball games, and to tour Santo Domingo—the first city built in the New World by European settlers—and its many cultural sites, including dozens of museums, botanical gardens and parks, the Columbus Lighthouse, the National Zoo, and the National Aquarium. Tourist activities include surfing, golfing, whale watching, scuba diving, bird-watching, biking, kiteboarding, and hiking. All of these diverse activities are supported by people working in the service industry. As the first place in the Americas visited by Christopher Columbus, the Dominican Republic is rich with historic sites and events. Santo Domingo is one of the places that claims to have the remains of Columbus—a man who traveled almost as much after he died as he did when he was living, because his body was moved many times. His history is a part of the history that intrigues many visitors.

In recent years, glamorous tropical resorts have been developed to attract more visitors. With the country's diverse environments ranging from desert to mountains to tropical rainforests, ecotourism—travel to areas of natural or ecological interest—is also increasing. The country has 16 national parks, and ecotourists enjoy all sorts of adventure, including scaling Pico Duarte, perhaps the most famous ecotourism destination in the Dominican Republic.

The economic impact of tourism is very important to the Dominican Republic. Tourism is a large and booming industry in this island country, employing everything from travel guides to baggage handlers, travel agents to hotel employees, and restaurant workers to fishing guides. It is estimated that the tourism industry is responsible for one out of every seven jobs in the country. Thus, the financial crisis and global recession of 2008 to 2009 had an immediate impact on the Dominican economy. The impact was less, however, than in many other tourist-dependent countries because the Dominican Republic is easy to reach from the United States and is relatively inexpensive. Airfare from Miami to Santo Domingo, depending upon season and schedule, is a quite reasonable $300 to $400. Additionally, prices for food, lodging, and other tourist-related activities are generally lower than in many other travel destinations.

TRANSPORTATION

Two major transportation systems operate in the Dominican Republic. One is run by the government, and the other is operated by private businesses. The government-operated system is primarily operated in Santo Domingo and Santiago, with costs being partially offset by public funds. Thus, the transportation costs are low for the consumer. However, much of this system is worn out and in need of repair and new vehicles. The private systems operate throughout the country, but with higher costs to passengers.

The country has more than 6,000 miles (9,656 km) of paved roads that serve as the dominant transportation network. Five major highways connect most of the country's towns, cities, and regions. Trains are rare, privately owned, and mostly serve the sugar plantations. Airports are located in Santo Domingo, Barahona, Santiago, La Romana, Puerto Plata, and Samaná. The facility at Santo Domingo serves as the country's chief international air gateway. Seaports also are important to the country's economy. Major ports are located in Boca Chica, Caucedo, Puerto Plata, Rio Haina, and Santo Domingo. The port of Santo Domingo is undergoing a major redevelopment that will integrate the port area and Santo Domingo's Colonial City to create an attractive destination for cruise ships and other high-end tourism.

COMMUNICATIONS

Communications come in many forms and most are readily available in the Dominican Republic. The country has nearly 1 million land phone lines and more than 5.5 million cell-phones. In 2008, six communications companies offered service throughout the country. The postal service is reliable, although often slow. Internet use has also advanced in the country, with nearly 2 million active users. The Internet country code for the Dominican Republic is .do.

Mass media is also important. The Dominicans can choose from 180 radio stations, 25 television stations, and more than 10 daily newspapers. The nation's cable company, Telecable National, provides many more television stations, as do satellite transmissions that provide many channels from Latin America and other locations around the world. Government regulation of the media has been abused in the past; however, even with rather strict oversight, today the government rarely interferes with television, radio, and newspapers.

ENERGY

The Dominican Republic has continually had problems related to its energy production and availability. Unfortunately, the country has very little domestic petroleum or coal. Thus, it has had two choices: depend upon importing these fuels from other countries or develop alternative energy sources such as hydro-electric power (power produced from the gravitational force of falling or flowing water, usually from a dam). Key dams that produce hydroelectric power are the Tavera Dam, completed in 1972, and the Sabana Yegua Complex, which opened in 1980.

Venezuela and Mexico have provided the Dominican Republic with oil at discounted prices because of the San Jose Pact. This agreement was put into effect in 1980 and guaranteed that Mexico and Venezuela would provide oil at discounted prices to Central American and Caribbean countries.

Other energy-related problems include frequent blackouts that can last for long periods. This problem is less frequent in tourist areas, as they have more reliable energy sources. Other problems that have plagued the energy industry include mismanagement, theft, low collection rates, and corruption. Some efforts are being made to correct these problems, but progress is slow. A law enacted in February 2009 made power theft against the law and promises to sentence violators with fines and prison. The lack of long-range planning to meet energy needs also plagues the country. This problem, however, may be addressed by the newly created Office of Energy Efficiency and Renewable Energy, which is under the National Energy Commission. This body is charged with creating new energy alternatives and planning for the future.

INTERNATIONAL TRADE

In the global age, the Dominican Republic is connected to the world by its trade of goods. As previously mentioned, the

For many years, the Dominican Republic has had problems related to its energy production. In 1994, the country was embroiled in controversy from its gasoline being brought over the border and sold on the Haitian streets (*shown above*). In 2009, Dominican residents clashed with the police when they demanded an end to chronic electricity shortages.

United States is the primary international partner for both exports and imports. Forty-six percent of the country's imports come from the United States, and two-thirds of its exports go to the United States. After the United States, the next leading trading partners for exports are Belgium and Finland. Export goods from the Dominican Republic include ferronickel, sugar, gold, silver, coffee, cocoa, tobacco, meats, and consumer goods. Imported products include food, petroleum, cotton and fabrics, iron, steel, machinery, chemicals, and pharmaceuticals. Besides the United States, import partners include Venezuela and Mexico, which provide oil.

The Dominican Republic is also a partner in various regional and global trade agreements and organizations. These include the Association of American States, which is a free-trade organization, and the Central America-Dominican Republic Free Trade Agreement (CAFTA-DR), which came into force in 2007. The CAFTA-DR is designed to boost investment and exports in the clothing industry. The country also is a member of the World Trade Organization, which supervises and works to open international trade. The Dominican Republic also belongs to the United Nations World Tourism Organization, which works to increase sustainable tourism for developing countries like the Dominican Republic, and the Organization of American States (OAS), which, in part, works to foster free trade.

ECONOMIC IMPACT ON THE LAND AND PEOPLE

As the country's lifeblood, the economy affects the people and land at all times. Citizens need jobs, transportation to their jobs, and basic necessities such as food, clothing, and shelter. Life in the Dominican Republic is significantly better than in Haiti but not as good as in the United States because of the depreciation of the Dominican peso against the U.S. dollar. Yet there is a silver lining. Many Dominicans who have immigrated to the United States send money to their families back home. Since many Dominicans use U.S. currency as much as their own, this amounts to millions of dollars each year and is a major source of revenue.

A major problem for people in the Dominican Republic is the wide gap in incomes and economic well-being. If you are wealthy, life is wonderful and your needs and wants are easily met. But if you are poor, as one-third of the population is, you struggle to have your family's daily needs met. As an example, the poorest half of the Dominican population receives 20 percent of the country's GDP, while the richest 10 percent receives a whopping 40 percent of the country's income. This gap leaves many living in poverty.

Economic activity also affects the land and environment. Many advocate for sustainable economic activity—that is, economic development that can be carried forward into the distant future without harming the environment. However, past patterns have left many countries, including the Dominican Republic, with an environment that has been scarred, poisoned, or otherwise degraded. Related problems faced by the Dominican Republic have included widespread soil erosion, damage to coral reefs, pollution of drinking water, acid rain, and deforestation. Some of these environmental problems, like deforestation, have been addressed in recent years (as mentioned, by replanting and setting aside land for national parks). Other problems, such as those related to mining, are still being solved.

7

Living in the Dominican Republic Today

What is it like to live in the Dominican Republic today? What are the benefits and burdens of being a Dominican resident? In this chapter, we take a look at the Dominicans today in order to better understand the people and their way of life.

A CULTURE IN TRANSITION

The Dominican culture has been flexible, influenced as it is by various domestic and foreign variables. Unless they are extremely isolated, cultures usually change as they adapt to new practices, interests, needs, and circumstances.

The arrival of the Spanish, first led by Christopher Columbus in 1492, signaled the start of many changes to the local culture. The Spaniards introduced many aspects of their own culture to the island.

These included their language and religion, food, class structure, and management systems. They also introduced a number of elements harmful to the local culture, including infectious diseases, forced labor, and torture. Thus, a culture can undergo change in ways that are either positive or extremely painful when forcefully imposed. From the time of the Tainos, Dominican culture has been evolving continually. Influences have come from many sources, including aboriginal, Iberian, African, French, American, and others.

During recent decades, Dominican culture has undergone yet another important and often difficult transition. It has gradually shifted from a traditional folk way of living to a more contemporary lifestyle deeply enmeshed in popular culture. A hallmark of this transition is a change from self-sufficiency, a lifestyle by which people provide for their own needs, to a modern economy and urban lifestyle in which people are dependent on others. You may have heard the terms *less developed* or *developing countries* and references to developed lands. Less developed countries or developing countries are not fully industralized and have less advanced financial, social, and legal systems and low standards of human rights guarantees for their citizens. Commonly called Third World countries, most have economies based on agriculture and citizens who earn poverty-level incomes. The countries contend with high inflation and debt and large trade deficits due to large loans from the World Bank (an international institution that offers loans to poorer countries). Despite their less advanced state, these countries want to do better socially and economically, and the levels of development may vary from one country to the next, with some developing countries having higher average standards of living than others.

Think for a moment of the way you live. How does it differ from the way of life experienced by an individual in a traditional society in some remote area of Asia, Africa, or Latin America? How many differences can you think of? One need not go back too many generations to find that many people in the Dominican Republic lived in a very traditional "folk culture" way. Today, most Dominicans at least aspire to enjoy the comforts and opportunities found in developed countries like the United States or the United Kingdom.

HUMAN DEVELOPMENT INDEX

While Dominicans are better off than many others in the Caribbean, they still have an economic situation far worse than people living in Canada and the United States. While basic needs are usually met, problems exist in daily life. In fact, the Dominican Republic ranks ninety-first on the Human Development Index (HDI), just about in the middle among the world's nations. The HDI is a measure of human well-being based upon several factors, including life expectancy, literacy, education, and standard of living. Among Caribbean countries, at least 10 rank higher than the Dominican Republic on the HDI. They include Barbados, Cuba, Jamaica, Trinidad and Tobago, and several smaller island countries. The Dominican Republic does fare much better than its island neighbor, Haiti. In fact, Haiti holds the lowest rank of any Western Hemisphere nation, a dismal one hundred fifty-eighth out of the 179 countries ranked.

Fortunately, living conditions in the Dominican Republic are far better today than in the recent past, and they continue to improve at an impressive rate. The key to human well-being is complex, but two conditions stand out if people are to thrive, prosper, and reach their potential as a society. First, the country must have a stable government that is responsive to the needs of the people. Second, a country must have a productive and growing economy. Fortunately, the Dominican Republic now appears to have both working in its favor.

HOUSING

The Dominican Republic faces a serious housing shortage. Poverty, of course, is one of the reasons that many people live

Migration to urban areas, rapid population growth, poverty, and destructive hurricanes have created a serious housing shortage. The need for living accommodations has led people to build houses made of wood, palm trees, and discarded materials with roofs of rusty tin sheets. In many cases, more than one family share a home.

in inadequate housing. Other important influences include the rapid pace of urban migration that has resulted in the explosive growth of nonrural populations. A second factor that affects housing and homelessness is the damage inflicted by severe weather, like Hurricane Georges in 1998. The fierce Category 4 storm was the second most destructive storm of 1998, affecting numerous countries, including Antigua and Barbuda, St. Kitts and Nevis, Haiti, the Dominican Republic, Cuba, the United States, and Puerto Rico—a commonwealth of the United States. In the Dominican Republic, Georges caused one billion dollars in damages and devastated nearly 10 percent of the country's housing from winds and flooding. A confirmed 438 people were dead or missing, about 155,000 people were left homeless, and damage to houses and public buildings reached an estimated $400 million.

Housing in the country consists of individual homes, single rooms, and apartments. Construction is usually done with concrete, wood, and palm. Compared to the cost of homes in the United States or Canada, housing prices are reasonable in the Dominican Republic. With significantly lower incomes, however, many people are unable to purchase homes.

EDUCATION

The level of educational attainment in the Dominican Republic is somewhat lower than in Canada and the United States. The literacy rate—the rate at which people are able to read and write—is 87 percent for Dominicans, whereas it is 99 percent in both Canada and the United States. The average Dominican attends school for 12 years, compared to 17 years of schooling in Canada and 16 in the United States. Schooling is free and required until the eighth grade. Only 59 percent of Dominican youngsters attend secondary schools after their required primary schooling.

The Autonomous University of Santo Domingo is the oldest institution of higher learning in the Western Hemisphere. It was authorized in 1538 after Pope Paul III ordered that a Dominican seminary become a university. Classes didn't begin until 1558. (The oldest university in the United States is Harvard, founded in 1636.) Today, the university has an enrollment of some 160,000 students, much larger than any university in the United States. More than two dozen other colleges and universities operate in the country today, about half of which are located in Santo Domingo.

HEALTH

Dominicans face a variety of health problems. Environmental problems such as water pollution and sanitation make the situation worse. Some of the diseases resulting from contaminated food and water include bacterial diarrhea, hepatitis A, and typhoid fever. Insect-transmitted diseases, including dengue fever and malaria, also affect the country's population.

AIDS has become the leading cause of death among teenagers and adults ages 15 to 49. Much of the HIV-AIDS problem is transmitted though the country's thriving prostitution and sex-tourism industry. The HIV-AIDS rate for Dominicans is 1.7 percent. More than 66,000 people are believed to be HIV-positive today, and each year about 4,000 people die from the disease.

Because Haiti and the Dominican Republic share many economic, migration, and health challenges, the two countries have mounted major joint health efforts, including mass vaccination campaigns and islandwide efforts to control tuberculosis. The two countries, along with the Red Cross, have agreed to work together on training community health workers, distribution of insecticide-treated bed netting in order to combat insect-transmitted diseases, home visits for those with HIV or AIDS, promotion of mother-child health, immunization, strengthening of water and sanitation infrastructure, and promotion of personal and collective hygiene methods.

CRIME

According to a 2009 crime and safety report from the Overseas Security Advisory Council, the Dominican Republic has seen an increase in the number of incidents of violent crime and other criminal activity such as robberies, home burglaries, kidnappings, car thefts, and credit card fraud. Although the following are some of the most beautiful cities, they are also the country's most violent: Santo Domingo, Hato Mayor, La Vega, Samaná, San Jose de Ocoa, and San Cristobal. The crime rate is attributed to unemployment, large-scale urban migration, increased drug and alcohol use, the drug trade, and the widespread availability of weapons. In addition, the Dominican Republic has served as a hub for Colombian drug operations that supply drugs to the United States and Europe.

Foreign visitors are attractive targets, and travelers should particularly be alert during power outages, as criminal activity is known to increase at such times. According to the U.S. Department of State, it is best to avoid isolated areas and to stay vigilant.

LIFESTYLES AND ACTIVITIES

Life in the Dominican Republic is filled with local cultural activities that can be entertaining and fun for residents and visitors alike. During holidays and celebrations, cultural treats like Dominican foods, music, and art are shared.

Holidays and Celebrations

Many Dominican holidays are centered on religious events that are tied to the Catholic Church. Christmas is the most celebrated holiday in the Dominican Republic. Trees are sold and decorated just as they are in North America. Many Dominican weddings are held during the Christmas season to tie in with the religious holiday. Most towns celebrate the patron Catholic saint who they believe helps to protect them and their community. These events are parties marked with music, foods, and other events. One popular Dominican patron saint is Our Lady of Altagracia (*altagracia* means "high grace") of Higuey.

Dominican legend holds that a treasured painting of Mary, the virgin mother of Christ, disappeared in the country shortly after two brothers had brought the painting from Spain in 1502. Amazingly, the painting later reappeared in an orange bush. The site of the bush was where the first church in Higuey was then built. Pope Pius XI decreed in 1922 that the Lady of Altagracia would be the spiritual mother of Higuey. The country's president then declared that January 21 would become a national holiday dedicated to the patron saint of Higuey. Today, nearly one million people make the annual pilgrimage to Higuey. And one of every 12 Dominicans is named Altagracia.

Many other holidays are also closely tied to the Catholic Church. They include Epiphany (January 6), Easter (March or April), San Juan Batista (June), and All Saints' Day (November 1). Religion, however, is not the only stimulus for holidays and celebrations for the Dominicans. Many others are designated to recognize important historical events. These occasions include Dominican Independence Day (February 26) and Duarte Day (January 26), which celebrates the birth of the founder of the Dominican Republic, Juan Pablo Duarte. Restoration Day (August 16) celebrates the war Dominicans fought against Spain from 1863 to 1865 to stop colonization. Columbus Day (October 12), of course, remains an important historical celebration in the country, with events held by his grave site in Santo Domingo.

Carnival

Perhaps the most anticipated holiday of the year is the famous carnival that is held in February. Throughout the country, this event features exuberant partying. Festivities include elaborate parades, pulsating music, festive dancing, vibrant costumes, spiritual masks, and other wild activities, all of which are flavored with Dominican culture. Major carnival events have been held during the entire month of February, ending on Independence Day (February 27), in Santo Domingo, La Vega, and Santiago since 1867. In fact, Santo Domingo's carnival dates back to the mid-1500s. La Vega's carnival is believed to be the oldest in the Dominican Republic—dating back even further than Santo Domingo's—with proof of carnival found in La Ruinas de la Vega Vieja (Ruins of the Old Fertile Valley). The people during that time disguised themselves as Moors (the Spanish term for Islamic persons) and Christians. During carnival, thousands of tourists flock to the country. The event provides them a great escape from cold winter weather in northern latitudes and a wonderful holiday celebration at the same time.

Carnival has been celebrated in the Dominican Republic since the 1500s. Each Dominican town offers their own twist on the event with colorful masks, costumes, characters, music, and dancing. Of the many costumes and characters, the most popular are the devils, or Diablos Cojuelos (*shown above*).

The Arts

Sharing Hispaniola with Haiti has allowed for some similarities in the arts, including music. Some music forms, like merengue, have Dominican roots that include Spanish and African influences. The traditional merengue is fast and often features some or all of the following instruments: maracas, saxophone, tambora drum, box bass, and accordion. Newer versions can feature electric instruments and incorporate other music forms such as salsa and rock and roll. The merengue rose out of the lower socioeconomic classes in the country and became popular during the reign of Trujillo (1930–1961). The music also translated into the dance steps that are also called merengue. Still very popular, the merengue is the national dance of the Dominican Republic. Other popular Dominican forms of music include bachata, which also rose out of the slums and rural areas, and Dominican rock, which has a distinctive sound.

Other music styles are popular in the country. They range from music imported from outside the country to local variations on existing styles of music. One of these is reggaeton (which originated in Panama and was popularized in Puerto Rico), a mix of American hip-hop and reggae, with a little bachata, merengue, and other Latin rhythms. A number of Dominican musical stars perform the country's popular musical forms. Some also find audiences far beyond the country's borders. Many of these are Dominican expatriates who live in the United States and other countries.

Art in the Dominican Republic began to develop its own styles after the country gained its independence in 1865. Thereafter, the Dominican lifestyle began to mix with the country's European heritage in paintings and other artwork. The country's African heritage also mixed this art style with images often inspired by folk tales, myths, and religion. Landscapes and portraits were also popular. In the twentieth century, imported styles such as impressionism and modernism influenced Dominican artists, who began to paint more realistic works showing images of the country and its people.

Traditionally, literature has been produced by the country's elite. With the elite tied to Spain and Europe, much of the literature has had a European flavor. However, authors like Julia Alverez are working and writing in a manner that leaves Spanish influences behind to create a Dominican style of literature. Even though she moved from the country to New York at the age of 10, she has sparked a Dominican style of writing that focuses upon local culture. Many of her works highlight the roles of women in the Dominican Republic.

THE DOMINICAN SPORT—BASEBALL

The answer—*El béisbol* !!! And the question is: What sport are Dominicans crazy about? Baseball is a major part of the culture in the Dominican Republic and the game has social, economic, and sometimes even political importance. Dominican baseball has also had a huge impact on the game in the United States and Canada, where Dominican players have become stars in the major leagues and legends back in their homeland. In 2006, one in seven major league baseball players in the United States was from the Dominican Republic. They include some of the best ballplayers playing the game today.

Since major league baseball was integrated in 1947, nearly 500 Dominican baseball players have played at the world's highest level. The first Dominican ballplayer was Ozzie Virgil, who arrived in the big leagues in 1956 and played for the Giants, Tigers, Orioles, and other teams. He has been followed by hundreds of other Dominican-born players. They include Albert Pujols, Miguel Tejeda, Manny Ramirez, David Ortiz, Pedro Martinez, Tony Abreu, Robinson Cano, Bartolo Colon, Vladimir Guerrero, Jose Valverde, and Jose Mesa.

Dominican stars from earlier decades are held closely in baseball lore with players like Juan Marichal; George Bell; Rico Carty; Julio Franco; Raul Mondesi; Sammy Sosa; and Felipe,

Matty, and Jesus Alou. Others such as Alex Rodriguez have a Dominican heritage and have lived on the island at times during their life. In 1983, Juan Marichal became the first Dominican elected to baseball's Hall of Fame in Cooperstown, New York. Today there are more Dominican baseball players in the major leagues than there are players from any other country, excluding the United States itself. In addition, nearly 30 percent of the professional players in the American minor leagues are from the Dominican Republic.

Why Are So Many Major League Players from the Dominican Republic?

Why do so many major league players come from the Dominican Republic? There are a number of reasons. First, the country has a genuine love for baseball, and youngsters play the game starting from a very young age. The game was originally brought to the Dominican Republic by Cubans who were fleeing a civil war that lasted from 1868 to 1878. Since its introduction, the game has become more popular here than anywhere else in the world. Today there are baseball fields even in the poorest communities, and hundreds of thousands of children fantasize about their chances of following other Dominicans and making it to the major leagues. Traditional hot spots for baseball prospects in the Dominican Republic have been places like Santo Domingo, San Cristobal, Bani, Nizao, Santiago, Cotui, and La Romana.

Second, baseball is seen by many as a way of escaping a life of poverty. Becoming a professional baseball player can provide financial security for the player's family. Star pitcher Pedro Martinez explained: "If you reverse time back 15 years ago, I was sitting under a mango tree without 50 cents to actually pay for a bus." This economic incentive is powerful. Major league teams have taken advantage of this financial situation; historically, they have paid many Dominican players less than their American counterparts.

Since the time that Cuban immigrants brought the game of baseball to the Dominican Republic, the sport has been the country's most popular pastime. Starting as a diversion during the down time of the sugarcane harvest, today the country produces the greatest number of players to go on and play professionally. In fact, all the major league teams have training camps in the country to scout and train players.

Today, all 30 major league baseball teams have academies in the Dominican Republic where they "mine" the country's youth for talent. While a few, like the stars mentioned earlier, go on to fame and fortune, many other players fail in their search for prosperity. Unfortunately, nearly all of them fall far short of realizing their major league dreams. According to sports agent Joe Kehoskie in the PBS documentary *Stealing Home*, which explores Cuban baseball and its effects on society and also mentions baseball in the Dominican Republic, the sad reality is that many young players sign for 5 or 10 cents on the dollar when compared to American players. The documentary also shows that many young Dominicans quit school between the ages of 10 and 12 to play baseball. A few of these academy players may make the major leagues, but more than 99 percent never play an inning in the big leagues. Thus, after being cut from the roster, they have no high school or college education to fall back on.

Third, major league baseball can sign contracts with Dominican players as young as 16. This allows players to be signed at a fraction of the cost of American players who cannot be signed until they are 18. Signing at such a young age, combined with the academy system, allows players to rise, if they are able, through the system to play in the minor and major leagues at lower salaries. The academies quickly develop the skills of rising players with a tight time schedule, proper diet, and lots of baseball; however, the academies are also places where alleged money kickbacks (money or favors given in secret to perform a certain action or for a referral that benefits the person who gave the money) often take place and inadequate players are thoughtlessly discarded.

Little League Baseball

With baseball's prominence in the Dominican Republic, it would seem likely that the country would also be prominent in the Little League World Series. Surprisingly, the Dominicans have been good but not great. In 1983, they were the runner-up, but this was the only time they reached the finals. This might be because many players become involved in the professional systems early. The Dominican Republic, however, was in the news in 2001 when an amazing pitcher, Danny Almonte Rojas, was found to be two years too old to be eligible for the series. Many forget that Almonte did not play for the Dominican team; rather, he was a member of the U.S. team. They had to forfeit all of the team's wins because of the ineligible player.

Dominican Baseball Leagues

Dominican baseball is not just a quest by talented athletes to get to the major leagues; it is also a game that is adored by fans. No other sport comes close in its popularity. The winter league is very popular and features many major and minor league players who want to improve their skills during the United States off-season. Six teams play in the winter league, with each playing a 50-game schedule that runs from October to December. Two of the teams are located in Santo Domingo, with others in Santiago, La Romana, San Pedro de Macoris, and San Francisco de Macoris. The top four finishers in the winter league then engage in a playoff series in January that results in a national champion being crowned by February. The national champion then goes on to play in the Caribbean Series with Puerto Rico, Mexico, and Venezuela. Other leagues also exist in the country, with some having ties to the major leagues.

Baseball Problems

Baseball in the Dominican Republic is not free of problems. Some of these problems have included financial kickbacks and injustices done to potential professional players. In addition, the steroid problem in major league baseball has also touched Dominican players in a major way. In 2009, Alex Rodriguez admitted that he had obtained steroids in the Dominican Republic, and Miguel Tejeda was convicted of lying about having used steroids. Too many Dominican players have shown that they will do what they believe is needed to achieve financial security and fame, even if it means abusing their bodies. Thus, Sammy Sosa's 600-plus home-run record has been tainted, as has Alex Rodriguez's quest to become the all-time home run record holder.

According to writer Tom Fish, 57 percent of Dominican players in the major leagues have tested positive for steroids. This is a rate far higher than that of players from any other country. Poverty may lead many to steroid use, but most players are also not aware of the effects of the drugs on their bodies. Obviously, education is required to reduce the use of steroids among young Dominican ballplayers.

CHANGING TIMES AND A CHANGING SOCIETY

As with all societies, the Dominican Republic continues to change. While historic Taino, Spanish, and African traditions form the foundation of the country's culture, many new elements are being introduced. Many of these new influences come from the Americas, including the United States, Latin America, and other Caribbean nations. Others come from faraway places such as China, Syria, Lebanon, and Japan, with each bringing new flavors to Dominican culture. Tourists also bring their cultures with them when they travel to the country. This has increased the amount of English spoken in the Dominican Republic. The globalization of cultures through mass media also brings foreign influences via the Internet, television, radio, movies, and publications. Thus, the Dominican Republic constantly changes with the times and reflects many new cultural elements in the daily life of its citizens.

CHAPTER

8

The Dominican Republic Looks Ahead

Many countries, especially those that have what they believe is a glorious history, tend to look to the past more than to the future. Certainly, the Dominican Republic has a long and honored history, but it also has experienced almost-constant social, political, and economic turbulence. During recent years, however, things have begun to change. Democracy seems to have taken root politically, and because of a more stable government, many social problems are being resolved and the economy is beginning to boom. Dominicans, more so than many of the world's people, have many reasons to look ahead with considerable confidence and optimism.

ENVIRONMENTAL ISSUES

Physically, the Dominican Republic has a number of challenges to its development. The tropical country has many miles of splendid

In 2009, the Dominican Republic, along with several global organizations, launched the Environmental Protection Program to work on environmental issues and enforce legislation to ensure proper protection of environmental quality and biodiversity. With 3 million visitors a year, tourism provides a strong incentive for environmental protection.

beaches and scenic mountainous landscapes. Only recently, however, have reliable access and adequate facilities begun to lure tourists to many of the country's nonurbanized areas. Both coastal and mountainous areas offer an excellent opportunity for further economic development. This is particularly true in regard to a growing ecotourism industry, in which people pay handsomely to experience nature in its raw state. Crystal-clear waters of the Atlantic and Caribbean also offer many recreational opportunities, as do offshore coral reefs.

A variety of environmental problems also beg serious attention. They include protecting soils from erosion, decreasing water and air pollution, and conserving forested areas. Stands of coastal mangrove must be preserved. These large aquatic shrubs with their stiltlike root system protect the shoreline from erosion and also create a valuable ecosystem for marine life.

When something occurs with great regularity, it is often said that it is like "death and taxes," two things that can be counted on to happen. For the Dominican Republic, this is true of hurricanes. Over time, many of these potentially treacherous storms have struck the island, often with devastating results. In a relatively poor country, financial resources limit what can be done to protect against such storms. Walls and roofs must be built to withstand storms, but this can be costly. Little can be done to protect crops—sugarcane, coconut palms, mangoes, papayas, and other plants susceptible to wind damage. Unfortunately, like death and taxes, Dominicans will simply have to endure such storms and their destruction as best they can.

PEOPLE AND CULTURE

During recent decades, population growth in the Dominican Republic has followed the trend of Latin America as a whole: The rate of natural increase (RNI) has dropped sharply. Today, the rate of population growth in the Dominican Republic no longer far outstrips economic growth. This means that on a per capita basis, Dominicans are better off financially than in the past. The current RNI of 1.5 percent is higher than the world average but not by a large margin. It is dropping rapidly and is somewhat lower than that of many less-developed countries. Looking to the future, it appears that the country's population growth does not pose a serious problem.

There is, however, a huge potential population problem lurking over the nearby western horizon. Haiti is the most desperate country in the Western Hemisphere. Its people are the poorest, its population density is one of the highest, and its economy is the weakest in the Americas. Its government is perhaps the most corrupt and ineffective in the hemisphere, and its environment is the most degraded. The country has few resources. It ranks at the bottom among countries of the Americas in the Human Development Index (HDI). For these reasons and others, it is little wonder that so many Haitians desperately want to leave their country. An estimated one million Haitians already have escaped the deplorable conditions of their homeland by migrating—mostly illegally—to the Dominican Republic. Were this trickle of people to become a flood, it would create a huge problem—socially, culturally, economically, and politically—for the country and its future.

Human development takes time and money. For example, schools, hospitals, and other social services require facilities and trained personnel. It will take time for the Dominican Republic to increase particularly secondary school attendance and the literacy rate. Both are essential to the country's future development. Health services, too, can be improved, with a resulting decrease in the country's infant mortality rate and increase in life expectancy.

The cultural options enjoyed by Dominicans continue to expand. As more and more people make the transition from a traditional, rural, folk culture to urban living, many more options are open to them. Particularly in Santo Domingo, but in other cities as well, people are becoming increasingly cosmopolitan. In a traditional society, everyone tends to look, think, dress, eat, and act the same. In contemporary culture, it is much easier for one to be different. Dominicans are becoming more global in their outlook through increased access to various types of media, including satellite television and the Internet, which literally places the world on one's television screen or computer monitor. Rapid and inexpensive transportation brings tourists to the island, and Dominicans can see the different ways that other people live. Dominicans also can travel to distant destinations, such as Miami or New York City, thereby broadening their global horizons. In a very real sense, a population that not long ago could best be described as being provincial remote islanders has taken its place within the diverse and cosmopolitan global community.

GOVERNMENT AND ECONOMY

Think for a moment about the various things that make your life comfortable, enjoyable, and rewarding. How many of the things on your list would you have if you lived in a country with a corrupt, ineffective government? Would your list be as long if you lived in a land of grinding poverty? There are so many things that we take for granted that many people can only dream about. We turn on the faucet and—voila—there is clean running water, both hot and cold. Used water and sewage disappear into systems where waste is treated. Turn on a power switch and the light, radio, TV, stove, air conditioner, heater, or other appliance works. You receive a public or private education and have access to the world's best health and medical care. You want to get someplace, and you are able to travel on a marvelous network of routes, whether by land, water, or air. Today, many (although not all) Dominicans for the very first time are beginning to experience many of the things that we accept as being normal.

Only during recent decades has the Dominican Republic had a responsible government that is responsive to the needs of its people. As the government has become increasingly democratic, people have been willing to invest in the economic development of their own land. Hand in hand, good government and economic growth go together. Politically, however, ample room exists for improvement. Cronyism, nepotism, and corruption continue to plague the political system, but conditions are improving. There is little reason to believe, however, that the Dominican Republic will ever revert to the politics of old. Sleazy dictators, government change by *coup d'etat*, military control, or periodic U.S. intervention appear to be things of the past.

Economically, there also exists ample room for improvement. In this context, however, we must look to the past if we

Although the Dominican Republic faces many challenges ahead in terms of social reforms, the country's economic progress promises great things for its future. Its stable economic and political environment, natural resources, beautiful architecture, advanced telecommunication system, and assortment of activities makes it one of the world's places to watch.

are to project into the future with any certainty. What once was a very weak and shaky economy has grown tremendously during recent decades. There is little reason to believe that such growth will not continue into the future, particularly after the current global economic recession has passed. Today, the Dominican Republic's economy is the second strongest within a region that includes not only the Caribbean Basin but also the countries of Central America (Panama northward to Gua-temala and Belize). In addition to its relatively new political stability, the Dominican Republic has a large and increasingly skilled workforce. Its proximity to the United States and Can-ada makes shipping relatively fast and inexpensive. Investment of foreign capital is increasing as potential investors sense that their resources will be safe and show a profit.

Perhaps the greatest potential for economic growth rests with the country's growing tourist industry. What kinds of things do most tourists expect when they visit a distant land?

Pleasant and efficient people who are able to fulfill their travel, visiting, entertainment, and other needs certainly are important. So are adequate facilities, such as efficient local travel, clean and adequate lodging, and clean restaurants. Enter-tainment, historical sites, cultural amenities also are important. Of greatest importance, people want to feel that they are safe. All of these conditions take time to develop, but the Dominican Republic has taken major steps to ensure that tourists to the country will have a safe and enjoyable experience.

Oh, yes, and during your visit to the Dominican Republic, you certainly will want to catch a baseball game. Who knows, you might be watching several future Hall of Fame inductees.

NOTE: All data 2009 unless otherwise indicated

Physical Geography

Location	One of the Greater Antilles, lying between the Caribbean Sea and Atlantic Ocean; occupies the eastern two-thirds of the island of Hispaniola, shared with Haiti
Area	Total: 30,242 square miles (48,670 square kilometers), slightly more than twice the size of New Hampshire
Boundaries	Border countries: shares 224-mile (360-kilometer) border with Haiti
Coastline	800 miles (1,288 kilometers)
Climate	Wet-and-dry tropical maritime, with little seasonal variation in temperature; sharp seasonal patterns of precipitation; northeast trade winds blow throughout the year
Terrain	Rugged mountains and highlands, with fertile lowland valleys and coastal plains
Elevation Extremes	Lowest point: Lago Enriquillo, 151 feet (46 meters) below sea level; highest point: Pico Duarte, 10,417 feet (3,175 meters)
Land Use	Arable land: 22.49%; permanent crops: 10.26%; other (mountain, woodland): 67.25% (2005)
Irrigated Land	1,708 square miles (2,750 square kilometers) (2003)
Natural Hazards	Lies within the middle of the hurricane belt and is subject to severe tropical storms from June to October; occasional floods and drought
Natural Resources	Nickel, bauxite, gold, silver; marine resources; some hydroelectric development; good soils
Environmental Issues	Water shortages, soil eroding into the sea and damaging coral reefs, deforestation

People

Population	9,650,054
Population Growth Rate	1.5% per year
Net Migration Rate	−2.22 migrant(s) per 1,000 population
Fertility Rate	2.76 children born per woman
Birth Rate	22.39 births per 1,000 population
Death Rate	5.28 deaths per 1,000 population
Life Expectancy at Birth	Total population: 73.7 years (male, 71.9 years; female, 75.6 years)
Median Age	Total: 24.9 years; male: 24.8 years; female: 25.1 years
Ethnic Groups	Mixed, 73%; white, 16%; black, 11%

Religions	Roman Catholic, 95%; other, 5%
Language	Spanish
Literacy	(People age 15 and older who can read and write) Total population: 87% (male, 86.8%; female: 87.2%)

Economy

Currency	Dominican peso
GDP Purchasing Power Parity (PPP)	$78 billion (2008 est.)
GDP per capita	$8,200 (2008 est.)
Labor Force	4.1 million (2008 est.)
Unemployment Rate	15.5% of total population (2008 est.) (rate of underemployment is much higher)
Labor Force by Occupation	Services, 65%; industry, 24%; agriculture, 11%
Agricultural Products	Sugarcane, coffee, cotton, cocoa, tobacco, rice, beans, potatoes, corn, bananas; cattle, pigs, dairy products, beef, eggs
Industries	Tourism, sugar processing, ferronickel and gold mining, textiles, cement, tobacco
Exports	$7.17 billion
Imports	$16.02 billion
Leading Trade Partners	Exports: U.S., 66%; Belgium 4%; Finland 3%; others, 27%. Imports: U.S., 46%; Venezuela, 8%; Mexico 6%; Colombia 5%; others, 35%
Export Commodities	Ferronickel, sugar, gold, silver, coffee, cocoa, tobacco, meats, consumer goods
Import Commodities	Foodstuffs, petroleum, cotton and fabrics, chemicals, pharmaceuticals
Transportation	Roadways: 12,144 miles (19,705 kilometers), of which 6,134 miles (9,872 kilometers) are paved; railways: 321 miles (517 kilometers); airports: 36 (18 with paved runways); seaports: Boca Chica, Caucedo, Puerto Plata, Rio Haina, Santo Domingo

Government

Country Name	Conventional long form: Dominican Republic Conventional short form: The Dominican Local long form: Republica Dominicana Local short form: La Dominicana
Capital	Santo Domingo
Type of Government	Democratic republic

Head of Government	President Leonel Fernandez (since August 16, 2004)
Independence	February 27, 1844 (from Haiti)
Administrative Divisions	31 provinces (provincias, singular–provincia) and 1 district* (distrito); Azua, Bahoruco, Barahona, Dajabon, Distrito Nacional*, Duarte, El Seibo, Elias Piña, Espaillat, Hato Mayor, Independencia, La Altagracia, La Romana, La Vega, Maria Trinidad Sanchez, Monseñor Nouel, Monte Cristi, Monte Plata, Pedernales, Peravia, Puerto Plata, Salcedo, Samaná, San Cristobal, San José de Ocoa, San Juan, San Pedro de Macoris, Sánchez Ramirez, Santiago, Santiago Rodríguez, Santo Domingo, Valverde

Communications

TV Stations	25 television stations (2003)
Radio Stations	181 (120 AM; 56 FM; four shortwave)
Phones	907,000 mainline telephones; 5.5 million cellular phones
Internet Users	106,000 Internet hosts with 1.7 million Internet users

3,000 B.C.	Ancestors of the Arawak Indian people settle on island of Hispaniola.
A.D. 1492	Christopher Columbus arrives at Hispaniola and establishes settlement.
1493	Christopher Columbus arrives on his second voyage to Hispaniola.
1496	Bartholomew Columbus forms settlement that later becomes Santo Domingo.
1505	First African slaves are brought to Hispaniola.
1506	Christopher Columbus dies in Spain.
1509	Diego Columbus, Christopher's son, is appointed governor.
1538	Autonomous University of Santo Domingo is established, the first in the New World.
1586	British admiral Sir Francis Drake captures Santo Domingo and forces Spain to pay a ransom to get the city back.
1591	Santo Domingo damaged by an earthquake.
1697	The Treaty of Ryswick signed,with Spain ceding the western third of Hispaniola to France.
1795	France gains control of all of Hispaniola.
1801	Haitian Toussaint L'Ouverture takes Santo Domingo from the French and gains control of the entire island.
1821	Dominican Republic separates from Spain.
1822	Haiti invades the Dominican Republic.
1836	Juan Pablo Duarte, a founder of La Trinitaria, leads a Dominican revolt against Haitian rule.
1842	Powerful earthquake hits Hispaniola.
1844	Dominican Republic becomes independent; first constitution adopted.
1848	Haiti invades the Dominican Republic but is driven out.
1855	Haiti invades the Dominican Republic again.
1860	Haitian fighting ends.
1861	President Santana declares that Spain is annexing the Dominican Republic.
1863–1865	War of Restoration reestablishes the independence of the Dominican Republic.
1869	Dominican Republic attempts to become a U.S. territory; U.S. Senate rejects the treaty by one vote.

1882	Ulises Heureaux elected president of the Dominican Republic for first time.
1899	President Ulises Heureaux assassinated.
1906	U.S. signs 50-year financial agreement with Dominican Republic.
1916-1924	U.S. uses Marines to occupy and stabilize the country.
1924	Dominican Republic gains independence from U.S.; Horacio Vasquez elected president.
1930	General Rafael L. Trujillo elected president, starting 31 years of dictatorial rule; Hurricane San Zenon hits the country and kills more than 2,000.
1937	Trujillo's Parsley Massacre kills more than 20,000 Haitians near border.
1956	Ozzie Virgil becomes first Dominican baseball player in the major leagues.
1961	Trujillo is assassinated.
1962	Military seizes power and overthrows President Joaquín Balaguer; free elections held, with Juan Bosch elected president.
1963	Bosch's government overthrown by the military.
1966	Balaguer elected president after years of economic decline and turmoil; new constitution instituted.
1972	Tavera Dam completed.
1979	Hurricane David strikes the country, killing nearly 1,000 people.
1983	Juan Marichal becomes the first Dominican elected to baseball's Hall of Fame.
1986	Balaguer elected president again and serves 10 more years.
1996	Leonel Fernandez elected president.
1998	Hurricane Georges strikes the Dominican Republic.
2000	Universal health care established in the country.
2002	Balaguer dies at the age of 95; constitution amended to allow two presidential terms.
2004	Leonel Fernandez elected president.
2007	Central America-Dominican Republic Free Trade Agreement (CAFTA-DR) enacted.
2008	Leonel Fernandez reelected president.
2009	El Metro begins operating in Santo Domingo.

Bibliography

Baker, Christopher. *National Geographic Traveler: Dominican Republic.* Washington, D.C.: National Geographic Society, 2008.

Borkson, Joseph L. (author) and Doug Gordon (editor). *Reflections on the Spanish Isle, Glories of the Dominican Republic.* Philadelphia: Cyrano Press, 2007.

Chandler, Gary and Liza Prado. *Lonely Planet Dominican Republic.* Victoria, Australia: Lonely Planet Publications, 2005.

Fodor's. *Fodor's Dominican Republic.* New York: Fodor's, 2008.

Harvey, Sean. *The Rough Guide to the Dominican Republic.* New York: DK Publishing, Inc., 2008.

Howard, John David. *Dominican Republic in Focus: A Guide to the People, Politics and Culture.* New York: Interlink Books, 1999.

Pons, Frank Moya. *The Dominican Republic: A National History.* Princeton, NJ: Markus Weiner Publishers, 1998.

Sauer, Carl O. "The Agency of Man on the Earth," in *Selected Essays 1963–1975, Carl O. Sauer.* Berkeley, CA: Turtle Island Foundation, 1981; pp. 330–363 [cited passage, 351].

Rogers, Lura and Barbara Radcliffe Rogers. *The Dominican Republic* (*Enchantment of the World. Second Series*). New York: Children's Press, 2008.

Brown, Isabel Zakrzewski. *Culture and Customs of the Dominican Republic.* Westport, Conn.: Greenwood Press, 2008.

Foley, Erin and Leslie Jermyn. *Dominican Republic* (*Cultures of the World*). New York: Marshall Cavendish Corporation, 2005.

Gallin, Anne, Ruth Glasser, and Jocelyn Santana (editor). *Caribbean Connections: The Dominican Republic.* Washington, D.C.: Teaching for Change, 2006.

Landau, Elaine. *Dominican Republic* (*True Books*). New York: Children's Press, 2000.

Ruck, Rob. *The Tropic of Baseball: Baseball in the Dominican Republic.* Lincoln, Neb: Bison Books, 1999.

Temple, Bob. *Dominican Republic* (*Discovering*). Philadelphia: Mason Crest Publishers, 2003.

Zuchora-Walske, Christine. *Dominican Republic in Pictures.* Minneapolis, Minn.: Twenty-First Century Books, 2007.

Web sites

About.com—Dominican Republic
http://geography.about.com/gi/dynamic/offsite.htm?site=http://www.info-please.com/ipa/A0107475.html
Geographic perspectives on the Dominican Republic.

Dominican Republic Ministry of Tourism
http://www.godominicanrepublic.com/
Official Dominican government site for tourism, which provides information on the history, geography, culture, and travel in the Dominican Republic.

Embassy of the Dominican Republic in Washington, D.C.
http://www.domrep.org/kids.html
Official Dominican government site provided for students in the United States, with extensive information on the country.

New World Encyclopedia
http://www.newworldencyclopedia.org/entry/Dominican_Republic
Site provides a comprehensive overview of the Dominican Republic,

including information about the history, physical geography, economy, and people

U.S. Department of State: Background Notes
http://www.state.gov/r/pa/ei/bgn/35639.htm
Official U.S. State Department site, which provides an overview of the history, economy, government, and other elements of Dominican society.

U.S. Library of Congress
http://rs6.loc.gov/frd/cs/dotoc.html
This site provides extensive information about the history, geography, economy, and other aspects of the Dominican Republic and other world countries.

Picture Credits

page:

  9: © Infobase Publishing
 13: © M. Timothy O'Keefe/Alamy
 18: © Infobase Publishing
 25: © Visual&Written SL/Alamy
 30: © John Mitchell/Alamy
 35: © North Wind Picture Archives/Alamy
 40: © Hulton Archive/Getty Images
 45: © Melanie Stetson Freeman/The Christian Science Monitor via Getty Images
 47: © Infobase Publishing
 49: © nik wheeler/Alamy
 53: © Nicholas Pitt/Alamy
 60: © RJ Lerich/Shutterstock
 63: © Ricardo Hernandez/AFP/Getty Images
 68: © STR/AFP/Getty Images
 73: © Simon Rawles/Alamy
 79: © Robert Sullivan/AFP/Getty Images
 85: © Wilmar Photography/Alamy
 90: © Vova Pomortzeff/Alamy
 94: © Andre Jenny/Alamy
 99: © Wilmar Photography/Alamy
103: © Alex Segre/Alamy

Index

Index

DOUGLAS A. PHILLIPS is a lifelong educator, writer, and consultant who has worked and traveled in more than 100 countries on six continents. From Alaska to Argentina and from Madagascar to Mongolia, Phillips has worked in education as a middle school teacher, administrator, curriculum developer, author, and trainer of educators across the United States and around the world. He has crisscrossed the world and has traveled in the Dominican Republic to better understand the country and its people.

Phillips has served as the president of the National Council for Geographic Education and he has received the Outstanding Service Award from the National Council for the Social Studies, along with numerous other awards. Phillips is a writer and serves as a senior consultant for the Center for Civic Education. He has written or co-written 18 books and has published numerous articles. In addition, he has trained thousands of people in numerous places, including New York City, Sarajevo, Ramallah, New Delhi, and remote African villages. His work has put him amid civil wars and social chaos to train people who are striving to promote democracy in their country. From his adventures and work with people from many cultures, he understands the importance, challenges, joy, and complexity of the world today. Phillips; his wife, Marlene; and their two sons, Chris and Daniel, live in Arizona; their daughter, Angela Phillips Burnett, lives in Texas.

Series editor **CHARLES F. GRITZNER** is Distinguished Professor of Geography Emeritus at South Dakota State University. He retired after 50 years of college teaching and now looks forward to what he hopes to be many more years of research and writing. Gritzner has served as both president and executive director of the National Council for Geographic Education and has received the council's highest honor, the George J. Miller Award for Distinguished Service to Geographic Education, as well as other honors from the NCGE, the Association of American Geographers, and other organizations.